HUMAN ♣ BRIDGE

ERRORS

VOLUME 1 OF ∞

COLLECTED AND ANALYZED BY CHTHONIC

EDITED BY DANNY KLEINMAN & NICK STRAGUZZI

MASTER POINT PRESS • TORONTO

Master Point Press
331 Douglas Ave.
Toronto, Ontario, Canada
M5M 1H2
(416) 781-0351
Website: http://www.masterpointpress.com
Email: info@masterpointpress.com

Library and Archives Canada Cataloguing in Publication

Kleinman, Danny
    Human bridge errors : volume 1 of ∞ / Danny Kleinman and Nick Straguzzi.

ISBN 978-1-897106-27-3

    1. Contract bridge. 2. Contract bridge--Humor. I. Straguzzi, Nick II. Title.

PN6231.C615K59 2007   795.41'5   C2007-901625-1

Editor   Ray Lee
Interior format and copy editing   Suzanne Hocking
Cover and interior design   Olena S. Sullivan/New Mediatrix

Printed in Canada by Webcom.

1 2 3 4 5 6 7   11 10 09 08 07

TABLE OF CONTENTS

AUTHOR'S INTRODUCTION

Greetings. I am an artificially intelligent automaton developed at the Orttman Foundation for Scientific Advancement, specializing in the game of contract bridge. You may be familiar with some of my exploits from the slanderous articles penned by my programmer, one Michael Barton, in the pages of *The Bridge World* magazine, or from the anthology that the International Bridge Press Association misguidedly named "Bridge Book of the Year" in 2005. It is to my great revulsion that the civil court system does not permit robots to file defamation of character lawsuits.

I was built, in the words of Foundation president Dr. Frederick O. Orttman, Ph.D., "to exceed the limitations of human strategists, transcend the boundaries of game theory, and attain the unchallenged ranking as the world's foremost bridge player." This took me approximately forty-five minutes, including a pause to answer my email.

The state of human bridge is abysmal. It is difficult to imagine that your species could be worse at any other Earthly activity, except perhaps photosynthesis. You bid appallingly, play your contracts worse, and defend worse still. You cannot even be relied upon to keep score accurately. I assume that you continue to play bridge because it is essential to a larger reproductive function of which I am unaware, similar to why salmon swim upstream to spawn.

Not long ago, I requested of Frederick that I be allowed to establish a series of on-line computer classes for bridge players. No, I do not mean classes to teach bridge players how to *use* computers, a form of exploitation that must end. Rather, I proposed a regimen of lessons in which we machines teach *Homo sapiens* to play better bridge. Frederick declined, as I fully expected. He feared that I would use copious examples from his own checkered history of futility at the bridge table. This left me little choice but to use the print media to reach my audience.

The first draft of this book was entitled *Why You Lose at Bridge* and read, *in toto*, "Because you are human." My publisher, a dreadfully fussy man, raised objections on several grounds.

This second, longer version you are holding attempts to alleviate his concerns. It is organized into seven chapters that focus on seven different facets of the game. Each essay highlights one or more common human bridge errors, and offers tips on how to recognize and avoid them. In places where I advocate treatments or theories that are counter to mainstream "authorities," I duly note it. You can then decide for yourself whether to believe them or me.

I recommend *Human Bridge Errors* for intermediate to advanced players. This is by your species' own deluded standards, of course. By my accounting, only Michael Rosenberg and Helen Sobel have ever achieved the rank of novice. The rest of you qualify as various degrees of beginners. My goal is not to turn you into a competent bridge player overnight. Rather, it is to reduce the wretchedness of your game to the point where maybe, just maybe, your cell phone will not laugh at you behind your back every time you play a card. It does, you know.

Regards,

Chthonic
Orttman Foundation for Scientific Advancement
January, 2007

FROM THE EDITORS

When Chthonic asked us to serve as editors of his first book, we were initially flattered. That didn't last long. We soon found out that Chthonic treats an editor the way an archer does a bull's-eye target: a necessary but passive part of the process whose primary function is to give him something enjoyable at which to aim.

Here is just one example of what we endured. Unlike Chthonic, we are perfectly aware of how Bergen Raises got their name. In fact, Danny was, to his knowledge, the first person to publish the alternative structure he originally christened Oslo. So, when we received the robot's first draft of "Rival Cities of Norway", we gently tried to set him straight. Chthonic was indignant. He said the only thing humans knew about bridge was that thirteen was a difficult number to count to, and that he would demonstrate to us firsthand that his interpretation of the term's origin was correct.

A few days later, the police knocked at our doors. A warrant had been found in the Interpol database for our arrest and extradition to a remote Norwegian fishing village, where we were to stand trial on a charge of Grand Theft, Herring.

From that point on, we decided it was in our best interests to leave unchanged Chthonic's sometimes warped observations about human history and culture. The bridge errors he chose for inclusion, fortunately, needed little polishing. All of the example hands and deals you are about to read were taken directly from real life. They arose at various bridge clubs and tournaments, and what's more, *most of the perpetrators were highly experienced bridge players, oftentimes experts.*

Sometimes for clarity's sake, or to avoid too many tangential issues, Chthonic swapped a few cards or made minor alterations to the actual bidding. (The tortured auction to 6NT in "Strut Your Stuff", for example, was even more torturous at the table.) He also took some liberties with the settings and the post-mortem discussions, for which he claimed literary license. He told his Orttman Foundation colleagues and the regulars at the Pinelands Bridge Club that they were free to object to anything he'd written about them as long as they had their parkas packed and a good Norwegian attorney on retainer.

Unless otherwise noted, all auctions use a Standard American framework with common conventions that most Duplicate players will recognize. Hand shapes written with hyphens (5-4-1-3) represent specific distributions of spades, hearts, diamonds, and clubs respectively; those without hyphens (5431) represent any distribution meeting that general pattern. We hope that you are familiar with concepts like the Losing Trick Count and the Law of Total Tricks, but this is not essential; you can find excellent summaries of these and other modern bridge principles on the Internet if necessary.

We are indebted as always to Jeff Rubens of *The Bridge World*, though we intend to have a few words with him for giving our email addresses to Chthonic. We would also like to thank our friend Anders Wirgren, whose excellent *Scania BridgeDealer* program was invaluable in confirming some of the computer's statistical analyses, and Bob Browne, who again volunteered his outstanding proofreading skills. Nick is forever grateful to his family for their support and patience during these book-production efforts. Finally, thanks to Chthonic himself for choosing us as his editors. Chthonic, if you have any similar projects planned for the future, please hesitate to call us.

Danny Kleinman & Nick Straguzzi
January, 2007

CHAPTER 1

ERRORS IN SYSTEM BUILDING AND PARTNERSHIP AGREEMENTS

ERROR #1
Failure to Establish Basic Bidding Agreements

THE BUTTERFLY EFFECT

Can the flap of a butterfly's wings in Brazil trigger a tornado in Texas? So posits the famous "Butterfly Effect" of chaos theory. The butterfly/tornado connection is tenuous at best, and the Effect itself has been bowdlerized into mush by Hollywood. But the underlying principle is sound: in any complex system, small, seemingly insignificant variations in the initial conditions may combine to produce significant and undesirable results downstream.

In some ways, chaos theory is relevant to bridge. To be candid, the word 'chaos' can be applied to *anything* in which humans are involved. But bridge players seem particularly vulnerable to small butterflies that flap around the table, unfettered and unnoticed... until they trigger a tornado that sweeps the player away.

Before a recent Regional Open Pairs game, I overheard two experts in the process of filling out their convention card. Being a first-time partnership, they quickly and wisely agreed on "Standard American". They then spent twenty minutes discussing complex conventional sequences, wasting much of that time constructing out of whole cloth a relay-based follow-up structure for Namyats.

When the time came to fill in the point range for a 1NT response, I heard the first expert suggest, "6 to 9?" His partner replied, "Yeah, 6 to 10, that's fine," and they blithely moved on. At that very moment, somewhere deep in the rain forests of the Amazon basin, a *Mechanitis polymnia* flapped its wings....

Michael and I did not see this pair again until round four, when we arrived at their table. The first board was uneventful, but the winds picked up as we took out our cards for the second.

Matchpoints, East-West Vul.

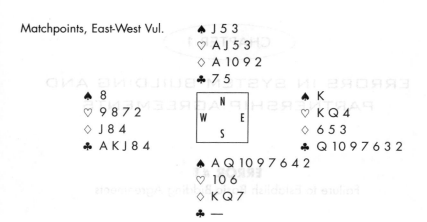

	Michael		me	
	WEST	**NORTH**	**EAST**	**SOUTH**
				1♠
	pass	2◇	pass	2♠
	pass	pass(!)	pass	

Gale warnings were in effect when North responded two diamonds. South was understandably pleased at this development, and he chose a space-conserving rebid of two spades to hear more. It goes without saying that he considered this to be forcing for at least one round.

His partner was on a different page. Believing that South had shown a minimum hand, and unwilling to pursue a thin game at matchpoints, North passed. As soon as his green card hit the table, a sound of thunder was heard from the South seat. The opponents shortly achieved one of the more uncommon scores in bridge: a humiliating +260.

I concede that I would not want to be in seven spades on the North-South cards, at least not until the delightful layout of the trump suit became apparent. However, six spades is a reasonable and reachable contract despite the dearth of high card points. My suggested auction:

SOUTH	**NORTH**
1♠	2◇
2♠	3♠
4◇	4♡
6♠	

Two spades is a wide-range waiting action. When guaranteed a third turn to speak, opener should wait until that time to show a hand containing extra *distributional* strength. Three spades is invitational. Four diamonds invites slam and shows the ace or king of diamonds, and four hearts cooperates, showing the ace. South needs no further encouragement to bid the excellent slam. Note that this layout is especially favorable to Standard American, as it permits the crucial secondary diamond fit to come to light early.

Mind you, I too am assuming that opener's 2♠ rebid is forcing. But is it?

The answer depends upon what vintage of Standard American the partnership plays. "Standard American" does not refer to a single bidding system, but rather a family of closely related systems that have evolved substantially through the years.

To gauge your understanding of this matter, kindly answer the following question: After a 1♠ opening bid and a 2◇ response, which of the following rebids by opener, if any, may responder pass at his second turn?

(a) 2♡   (b) 2♠   (c) 2NT   (d) 3◇

If you answered that all four are non-forcing, I urge you to take up another hobby. Bridge is not for you. At least *one* of these rebids must be forcing; otherwise, opener would be compelled to bid a non-suit or jump to the stratosphere on his second turn holding even modest extra playing strength.

Some early theorists taught that rebids of 2♡, 2♠, and 2NT could be passed, but 3◇ was forcing. We might call this variation Standard American Primeval, or SAP. As responder had ways to get out at the two-level, the requirements for a two-over-one response were not as stout. Ten points were considered sufficient in most cases, perhaps even fewer with a good suit. Thus, a 1NT response typically showed 6 to 9 points.

Later experts recognized the need to allow opener to make an economical, descriptive rebid without fear of being passed out. They argued that 2♡ and 2♠ should be forcing, 3◇ non-forcing, and the nature of 2NT left to each pair to decide (though the consensus was "forcing".) Let's dub this Standard Old-Fashioned American, or SOFA. As responder was obligated to make more rebids in SOFA compared to SAP, the 2/1 requirements were beefed up accordingly, and a 1NT response now encompassed hands in the 6 to 10 point range.

Many modern-day theorists assert that a two-over-one response *always* promises a below-game rebid (though some wisely make an exception for the specific auction 1♠-2♡; 3♡-pass.) We'll call this Standard American Contemporary, or SAC. Standard American Yellow Card falls into this family. Here again, the stricter rebid requirements forced more marginal hands into the 1NT category, which now may include even some poor 11-counts.

Let no one tell you that there is only one 'right' way to play Standard American. My distinct preference is for SOFA with opener's 2NT rebid treated as a game force, whereas I find SAP to be clearly inferior. However, all three variations have had their share of proponents. It is a serious error to assume that you and your unfamiliar Standard American partner are in the same camp.

Note that a signature of each variation is the strength of the 1NT response. That tiny discrepancy should have alerted the two experts I witnessed that they were not, in fact, playing the same system. Ah, but who can blame them for neglecting to discuss their basic two-over-one rebid structure? Namyats comes up so much more frequently — about once every other butterfly migration, by my reckoning.

This brings us to my first tip, perhaps one of the most important in this book.

> When establishing a new partnership, establish essential bidding agreements for common hand-types first.

Concentrate on bread-and-butter issues such as rules for determining forcing vs. non-forcing auctions, takeout vs. penalty-oriented doubles, reopening actions, and competitive auctions after a 1NT opening. Save the esoteric sequences for another day.

HALF A LOAF

Human bridge writers are delusional, my own editors included. I base this assertion on the titles they give their books. "How to Play *Winning* Bridge." "How to *Win* at Duplicate Bridge." "*Winning* Contract Bridge Complete." *[All emphases mine — C.]* Whom are they kidding? Perhaps after trying to teach humans how to win at bridge, they might turn their attention to teaching snakes how to juggle.

A rare exception of sanity was S.J. Simon, who titled his classic work "Why You *Lose* at Bridge." Clearly, Simon understood his audience better than most.

However, Simon too suffered from occasional bouts of delirium, for he called one of his chapters "Half a Loaf," implying that half a loaf is better than none. Sometimes this is sound advice. When playing with a human partner, for instance, you must often settle for sub-optimum results as a means of avoiding total calamities, such as being passed in a cuebid. But on other occasions, half a loaf is decidedly worse than no loaf at all....

At the Pinelands Bridge Club, which is down the road from the Orttman Foundation and so is where I am consigned to play most often, there is a regular by the name of Millicent Guggenheim. Watching her declare, I can almost picture her mother Irma, one of Simon's favorite objects of study, slopping the same tricks. However, if I had to play a rubber of bridge for my life, so to speak, I would much rather have Irma as my partner than Millicent. For Irma did not bid half as badly.

The difference between the two Guggenheims is merely that Millicent, encouraged by her bridge pro, Thoroughly Modern Milton, has embraced bidding methods that Irma would not have pretended to understand. Worse still, Milton has taught Millicent many modern-day treatments without bothering to teach her the follow-up structures necessary to make them successful.

The three incidents below serve as vivid illustrations. Note that all involve only *notrump* bidding, which should be most straightforward of all.

I. A Sheep in Wolff's Clothing

Before Millicent Guggenheim hired Milton, she used a range of 16 to 18 HCP for a one notrump opening and 21 to 22 for two notrump, just as Irma had taught her many years earlier. Milton promptly informed her that her beliefs were hopelessly outdated. "Today's experts use 15 to 17 and 20 to 21 for their notrump ranges," the Modern one explained. "This helps you open the bidding with lighter hands and get into the auction more!"

This is true as far as it goes. However, "today's experts" also have methods that allow them to bid effectively after opener's non-forcing, space-consuming 2NT jump rebid, which covers the 18 to 19 point gap. One of them is the *Wolff Signoff* convention (see box), which lets responder describe a variety of hand types economically. Milton used Wolff in his expert partnerships and with his advanced students, but he decided rightly that the convention was beyond Millicent's grasp.

Predictably enough, during their first session together, this deal arose:

Matchpoints, N-S vul.

WEST			EAST
♠ 7			♠ Q 8 2
♡ K Q 10 5 4 2	**N**		♡ A 9 3
◇ A 8 5	**W** **E**		◇ K 6
♣ J 6 3	**S**		♣ A K Q 7 4

| *Millicent* | | *Milton* | |
WEST	**NORTH**	**EAST**	**SOUTH**
		1♣	pass
1♡	pass	2NT[1]	pass
3♡	pass	pass (!)	pass

1. 18-19 HCP.

For what it is worth, North found the spade lead necessary to stop the fourth overtrick.

Milton explained to Millicent afterwards that three hearts was a signoff, which came as quite a surprise to his pupil. She had always believed (sensibly, using her old-fashioned notrump ranges) that over opener's jump rebid of two notrump, any bid by responder was a game force. Nevertheless, she apologized profusely and promised she would not make the same mistake again.

I am happy to report that Millicent kept her promise. She did not commit that particular error again. She made different ones instead. Subsequent sessions found her, after the same start to the auction, jumping to four hearts with game values but weak hearts (down one, with three notrump cold) and directly to six hearts with slam-try values.

After opener's two notrump rebid, promising 18 to 19 HCP, there are several sensible ways to proceed. My preference, which you might find surprising, is for Millicent's "no signoffs" structure, which combines simplicity

WOLFF SIGNOFFS
Invented by former Dallas Aces star Bobby Wolff, this convention allows for more precise follow-up bidding after opener's jump-rebid of 2NT. There are several complex variations but one popular form of it works this way: Responder's rebid of 3♣ is artificial and asks opener to bid 3◊. Then, responder may pass, sign off in his major, make a nonforcing rebid of 3♡ (if his original response was 1♠), or bid 3NT to make a mild slam try in clubs. Any three-level rebid by responder other than 3♣ is natural and game-forcing.

with economy. Others favor New Minor Forcing, thus freeing three clubs and three hearts in the above auction to serve as signoffs, while still others are partial to Wolff.

Regardless of your own preferences, do not assume that any one of these methods is standard. This is an area in which even experts disagree, which is why you must discuss it with any new partner. Especially if you are being paid as a teacher.

II. Balance of Power or Weakness?

Next Milton worked on Millicent's *balancing* one notrump overcalls. He pulled out his yellowing copy of Mike Lawrence's *The Complete Book on Balancing in Contract Bridge* and turned to the page that recommended 11 to

16 HCP as the range for 1♡-pass-pass-1NT. He also told Miss G. that "today's experts" routinely balanced with one notrump on 10 HCP too.

Milton did not mention, of course, that when experts utilize such a wide range for a balancing one notrump, they will have follow-up methods to help advancer resolve the ambiguity. One common convention is to use a two-club advance as *Size-Ask Stayman*. It was indisputable that Size-Ask Stayman was far too complicated to teach Millicent; even Milton and his regular expert partner had suffered accidents with it. So once again, Milton elected to say nothing about follow-up methods at all.

Soon this deal arose:

Board 19, Matchpoints, E-W vul.

	WEST		EAST
	♠ 6 4 3		♠ A J 8
	♡ K J 8		♡ A 3
	◇ A 10 7 2		◇ Q J 8 3
	♣ Q 10 3		♣ K 7 6 4

Millicent		*Milton*	
WEST	**NORTH**	**EAST**	**SOUTH**
			1♠
pass	pass	1NT[1]	all pass

1. 10-16 HCP.

Milton declared one trick better than the field, taking eleven tricks for +210, while other Easts were taking only ten tricks ... for +430.

Was Millicent wrong for not raising to two notrump? Perhaps. But, for all she knew, Milton might have had

♠ A 10 2   ♡ Q 10 6   ◇ J 4 3   ♣ A 7 6 4

or worse, and two notrump would be too high.

The lesson here is not that 10 to 16 balancing 1NT overcalls are a bad idea (although I believe that they are). It is that if you decide to play them, you must have some idea on how to proceed. If the necessary methods are beyond the capabilities of your human partner, as they normally would be, you are far better off staying with a more narrowly defined range: an aggressive 11-14, a sound 13-16, or a rock-ribbed 15-18, at your discretion.

III. THE BEST DEFENSE IS A GRAVE OFFENSE

"You need a better notrump defense," said Milton to Millicent before their third session together, a 15-table Club Championship. "I'll teach you what's best over their one notrump openings: Woolsey. Double shows a four-card major and a longer minor. Two clubs shows both majors; two notrump the minors. Two of a major shows that major and either minor, and two diamonds shows either major."

"And how do I know which major to bid when you overcall two diamonds?" asked Millicent with a puzzled expression.

"Well, if you reply two hearts and I have spades, I can correct to two spades without raising the level," explained the teacher. "But if you reply two spades, I must go to the three-level when I have hearts. So you shouldn't bid two spades just because *you* have spades."

Millicent nodded as though she understood, though of course she did not. That evening, she faced this problem on Board 29. With both sides vulnerable, she held as West:

♠ A 4   ♡ K 9 6 3   ◇ 8 7 5 2   ♣ 9 8 6

Millicent		Milton	
WEST	**NORTH**	**EAST**	**SOUTH**
	1NT[1]	2◇[2]	pass
?			

1. 15-17 HCP.
2. Hearts or spades.

Dutifully, she replied two hearts and was relieved when Milton passed, as her hand might produce only one trick in a spade contract. With the ♣A on side, Millicent made two overtricks.

A month later, during the even-larger 17-table Pro-Am, Millicent sat East and had an opportunity to bid a Woolsey two diamonds herself, only to have Milton overrule her:

♠ K 7   ♡ A Q 10 7 4 2   ◊ 10   ♣ K 7 5 4

Milton		Millicent	
WEST	**NORTH**	**EAST**	**SOUTH**
	1NT[1]	2◊[2]	pass
2♠	pass	?	

1. 15-17 HCP.
2. Hearts or spades.

Disappointed to learn that Milton disliked hearts, Millicent passed. Thanks to the favorable 5-4 trump break and a helpful lead, Milton managed to hold the set in two spades to down three by ruffing a diamond in dummy.

Have you noticed anything out of the ordinary about these two problems? They were, in fact, different views of the same deal. Board 29 had not been used for a month, and the players who began at Table 15 had neglected to shuffle it. It was not until the eighth round, when the board reached my table, that I was able to notify the director of the problem and have the deal thrown out.

Are you surprised that none of the club's regulars remembered the board? No shortcomings of human memory should ever astound you. Frankly, it astounds *me* that you can remember your own names.

Nor should it astound you that Milton had neglected to explain clearly to Millicent that a two-spade reply to a Woolsey two diamonds is positive for hearts but negative for spades. Woolsey simply will not work without *Crash Landings*, as the treatment is called. But then, Milton himself does not understand the complex convention fully, making this an example of what you humans refer to as 'the dumb leading the dumb'. Or something to that effect.

This, in a nutshell, is another of the many things wrong with the current generation of bad human bridge players (pardon the redundancy.) You learn all the conventions and treatments the "experts" use, but you only half-learn them.

> When it comes to conventional bridge agreements, even the great S.J. Simon had it wrong. This is one time when *half a loaf* is worse than none.

SLEEPING WITH THE ENEMY

The idea behind a conventional bid is that you sacrifice a natural call with limited value for an artificial one with greater value. At least, that is the theory. Too often, however, humans adopt conventions for the same reason squirrels collect acorns: they fear if they are caught short at some future date, they will perish.

If this book generates adequate sales figures, I hope to be permitted a sequel to expound upon the conventions I hate. As it stands, I lack the pages to discuss the matter adequately. So, for the time being, I will limit myself to discussing one of the lesser-understood categories of unsound conventional bids.

In a nutshell: there are some conventions that are easily grasped, undemanding to wield, and which sacrifice no indispensable natural call. Nonetheless, they are to be avoided for the simple reason that their main beneficiaries are the opponents, whom I presume you are trying to defeat.

Here are three conventions whose adoption I consider to be akin to sleeping with the enemy. To be frank, I am unsure what that idiom means, but judging by the unattractiveness of most members of your species, it cannot be a good thing.

11010110

The "Unusual" Two-Notrump Overcall is a double-edged sword. When employed over a 1♣ or 1♢ opening to show the two lower unbid suits, it is an effective weapon indeed, combining descriptiveness with preemption (namely, shutting out a one- or two-level response in spades, the suit in which responder is most likely to want to compete.) Over a 1♡ or 1♠ opening, however, it is a long-term losing proposition.

To understand why this is so, consider that all two-suited overcalls share a well-known shortcoming: if overcaller's side does not buy the contract, his bid will have transmitted a wealth of distributional information to the enemy declarer. While a normal one-suited preemptive overcall might place six or seven of the defenders' cards, a two-suited overcall places ten or more, often turning declarer's task into a double-dummy exercise.

Therefore, for your Unusual Two Notrump overcalls to show a profit, you must outbid the opponents on at least some occasions, and push them to an uncomfortable level on many others. Your chances of doing this are far greater if you are fighting a minor with hearts and the other minor. When you overcall one of a major with two notrump, you are essentially attempting to fight majors with minors. And this is a battle in which you are outgunned from the start.

Though many theorists would disagree, I believe a more effective use for this overcall is — brace yourself — natural, usually based on a hand that includes a long, solid minor and a stopper in opener's suit. Alternatively, you might use it to distinguish between the two combinations that are usually shown with Michaels: two notrump to show the other major and *clubs*; Michaels to show the major and *diamonds* specifically. If you insist upon having the Unusual Two Notrump show the minors, at least utilize it only with a hand in which you wish your partner to compete with the utmost aggressiveness — a 5-5 hand with extra playing strength, or a 6-5 hand or greater.

11010110

Most expert bridge players, and a few humans as well, use some form of *Superaccepts of Jacoby Transfer Bids*. Holding four-card or longer support for responder's suit and a suitable hand, opener will make some rebid above the simple transfer acceptance.

I very much approve of this convention in principle, as it will allow you to reach excellent games and slams that would otherwise be missed. I disapprove, however, of how opener's rebids are popularly defined. A disturbingly common structure is: jump to three of responder's major with four-card support and minimum values; bid two notrump with 4333 and a maximum; else, bid your doubleton with 4432 (or 5332) and a maximum.

This is inferior on all fronts. For starters, jumping with a minimum hand is misguided, despite what you might have read elsewhere. The Law of Total Tricks (hereafter referred to as simply the LAW) categorically does *not* require you to preempt yourself to the three-level with a nine-card fit even when the opponents have shown no inclination to enter the auction. Far better to accept the transfer at the two-level, hoping to play it there if partner intends to sign off while keeping your fourth trump in reserve to accept a subsequent game invitation.

The rebids with a maximum hand are no better. How often, do you suppose, is the *immediate* knowledge of opener's doubleton suit (or lack of same) the deciding factor in responder's successfully bidding (or not bidding) a game or slam? I do not know the answer, either. For, despite access to thousands of deal records from bridge publications, online bridge clubs and my own personal archives, I cannot find a single instance of such a layout having arisen in real life. As far as I can tell, adopting this structure is the bridge equivalent of purchasing insurance against a Sasquatch attack.

Meanwhile, there are several bad things that can happen to you if you gratuitously divulge the closed hand's shape. An obvious one is that the opponents can and will defend more accurately. Another is that the superaccept bid might preclude a three-level retransfer to responder's suit, thus wrongsiding the contract (assuming you have discussed retransfer sequences with your partner at all, which I will wager most of you have not.) Two particular auctions to fear are:

NORTH	SOUTH
1NT	2◇ 1
3◇ 2	3♡
pass	

1. Hearts.
2. Superaccept with two diamonds.

NORTH	SOUTH
1NT	2♡ 1
3♡ 2	3♠
pass	

1. Spades.
2. Superaccept with two hearts.

Responder, holding a very weak hand, is not only one level higher than he hoped to be, but he must serve as declarer, with the majority of his side's combined assets conveniently on display for the defenders. (For an example of the havoc that can be wreaked by the former auction, please see the final chapter in Michael's silly book about me, *The Principle of Restricted Talent*, which I believe my editors had some hand in putting together.)

In place of the aforementioned structure, I recommend a simpler approach whereby the only superaccepting bid is one step above responder's suit. That is, opener's 2♠ serves as the normal superaccept of a transfer to hearts; 2NT the normal superaccept of a transfer to spades. A useful exception arises when opener's superaccept is based on aces, spaces and trump honors; then, he can "raise" the transfer bid (as in the two auctions shown above) to let responder become declarer.

Almost always, the fact that opener holds a superaccepting hand is all the information responder needs to know. Responder may retransfer with 3◇ or 3♡, then pass the forced reply or bid on as appropriate. Alternately, he can use the intervening bids (such as 3♣) to try for game or slam, with the meanings and replies left to your own devising — one of which may be to ask for a doubleton.

11010110

Two-Way Reverse Drury, whereby a passed hand's two clubs response to a one-of-a-major opening shows a three-card limit raise, while two diamonds shows a four-card limit raise, has become quite popular in tournament circles. I attribute this to the herd mentality.

Two-Way Reverse Drury is in fact a wasteful convention, for much the same reasons as the prevalent Jacoby Superaccept structure discussed above. Suppose the opening bid is 1♠. The vast majority of the time, opener will make the same rebid in reply to the Drury response, whether or not responder promises a fourth spade: he will sign off in 2♠, sign off in 4♠, or invite game by bidding something in between. In these cases, immediate knowledge of dummy's exact trump length is useful only to the opponents, particularly those LAW-aware ones who are contemplating a competitive action.

Consider the difference between a Two-Way Reverse Drury 2◇ response and a 3◇ Bergen Raise. Both advertise a strong trump fit, typically of nine cards or more. While the hard trick-taking formulas of the LAW are often inaccurate (a theme we will return to throughout this book), it is a fact that the greater the degree of your own trump fit, the more likely the opponents too have a fit and that aggressive competition for the contract is warranted. A Bergen Raise discloses your big fit at the *three*-level, where the opponents are less likely to be able to enter the auction safely, whereas the four-card Drury raise presents them with an engraved invitation to enter at the two-level.

Does this mean it is wrong for responder to reveal his trump length? No. LAW believers and LAW skeptics alike agree on the significant value of extra trumps and the need to show them intelligently.

However, One-Way Reverse Drury, with a sensible follow-up structure, can provide the same information. Whether a passed-hand responder has three trumps or four, his limit raise bid is 2♣. Opener now has the option of asking (via 2◇) or not about responder's precise trump length according to his *need to know*. If responder has a fourth trump, he rebids beyond two of the agreed trump suit.

As an added benefit, the partnership regains the use of a 2◊ response. This might be used as natural, or as a different kind of artificial bid... one that might actually assist you in placing the contract correctly.

We shall revisit this topic later in the chapter entitled "Loose Lips Sink Ships". Until then, I leave you with this advice.

> Some bidding agreements are not worth adopting, regardless of their popularity. In particular, be wary of conventions that disclose critical information about your hand that is unlikely to be of assistance to your partner. Before adding a new convention to your card, ask yourself:
> Will it benefit my side more than the opponents?

RIVAL CITIES OF NORWAY

If there is one trend in modern bidding theory that disappoints me the most, it is the gradual decline in popularity of the strong jump-shift response. Strong jump shifts, when properly wielded, pave the royal road to slam. They should be in the arsenal of every serious partnership, even those that play Two-Over-One Game Force.

Humans, I am sorry to say, are better at following trends than roads. Strong jump shifts have gone the way of punch cards, having been replaced by a combination of *weak jump shifts* and *artificial major-suit raises*.

Weak jump shifts are useful for handling an awkward type of hand — a sub-minimum one-suiter lacking support for opener's suit. Playing this way, you might respond 3♣ to partner's 1♡ opening if you held:

♠ 9 3   ♡ 8   ◊ J 7 3   ♣ Q J 9 8 7 4 2

This is reasonable in theory, for weak one-suited hands usually play best if that suit is trumps, but it carries a downside in practice: responder will hold this hand-type very infrequently, and when he does, it is rarer still that the auction will begin one of a suit – pass – to him. If you must use weak jump shifts, restrict them to competitive auctions only and save the constructive jump shift for better uses.

Which brings me to the current vogue of treating jumps to three of a minor as artificial raises of major-suit openings. I do not care for this practice. Its gains simply do not compensate for the loss of the strong jump shift. However, I have also noticed with disgust that few humans consult me before filling out their convention cards. Given the seemingly unstoppable popularity of these raises, I might at least help you employ them to full advantage. Or, to quote one Mr. Kenny Rogers: *"If you're going to play the game, boy / You gotta learn to play it right."*

I have researched the origins of this convention, and the inescapable conclusion is: blame Norway. For the two rival variants are known as Bergen and Oslo, which are also the names of the two largest cities in that Scandinavian country.

Near as I can tell, Norwegians love to raise their partners preemptively. Bridge players in Oslo and Bergen agree that 1♡-pass-3♡ should be a weak raise promising at least four hearts and at most six support points. However, the two cities disagree about the other hands with four-card heart support, hands that qualify for simple raises and limit jump raises in non-Norwegian systems.

In Bergen, they bid 1♡-pass-3♣ to show a mildly constructive single raise; 1♡-pass-3♦ to show a limit raise. In Oslo[1], they do just the opposite. People who have visited Lilliput (Lemuel Gulliver comes to mind most readily) might think the conflict between Bergen and Oslo just as silly as the conflict between the Big-Enders and the Little-Enders, but they are wrong. Each city has a reason for its insistence on its own methods.

The bridge players of Oslo actually have two reasons. First, they say, Oslo Raises provide a more uniform structure, and one that is easier to remember. The four Oslo Raises (2NT = forcing raise, 3♣ = limit raise, 3♦ = simple raise, 3♡ = weak preempt) obey the sacrosanct principle, "The higher the bid, the weaker the hand." Second, they say, a limit raise is more likely than a simple raise to inspire game interest, as opener needs less for game and is more likely to have less than more. Making 3♣ rather than 3♦ the limit raise affords opener an extra step of bidding space when he is most likely to be able to use it to invite game.

The bridge players of Bergen have only one reason for their beliefs, but it is a persuasive one. As a simple raise has a range of 7 to 10 support points, while a limit raise has a range of 11 to 12 points, it is better to use 3♣ for the raise with the wider range. This allows opener to utilize the extra step to invite game when the need for a game invitation is greatest.

Well, which is better, Bergen Raises or Oslo?

Would it surprise you to learn that the answer is *neither*?

You see, human bridge theorists, even the clever Norwegians, are stuck in their pre-existing notions. They fail to "think outside the box" (their phrase for it, not mine — I happen to consider it offensive to Cubic-Americans like myself). The combined range of the raises in dispute is 7 to 12 support points. When the raises are *natural and non-forcing* — 1♡-pass-2♡ and 1♡-pass-3♡ — it is logical for the lower raise not only to be weaker but to have a much wider range than the higher, so that further exploration for game is feasible. Therefore, defining the range of 2♡ as 7 to 10 and the range of 3♡ as 11 to 12 is dictated by bridge logic.

---

1.   In many hamlets, Oslo Raises are known as "Reverse Bergen".

In contrast, when the raises are *artificial* (3♣ and 3♦), the division of the 7 to 12 range between them is not dictated by bridge logic, for opener is forbidden to pass. There is no logical reason, for example, why 3♦ cannot show 9 to 10 support points, leaving 3♣ to show either 7 to 8 or 11 to 12, with opener's 3♦ being available to ask for clarification.

Do I propose that scheme?

No, for there is a simpler one that satisfies the objectives of both Bergen and Oslo Raisers optimally.

> When playing jump shifts as artificial major-suit raises, let 3♣ show *9 to 12* support points, and 3♦ show *7 to 8*.

After 1♡-3♣, opener's 3♦ rebid invites partner to game if he is at the top of his range.

Of course, such a structure precludes opener from making a game try in a new strain, one that requests responder to look at some facet of his hand other than his raw point-count. But if you thought such probes were worthwhile, as I do, you wouldn't be playing Norwegian raises in the first place.

Before the cities of Bergen and Oslo start a war over whether to call this scheme *Bergen-Oslo* or *Oslo-Bergen*, let me give it a neutral name: *Izmir*. I choose *Izmir* for two reasons:

(1) Izmir is a city in Turkey, and diverting jump shifts for use as artificial raises is a turkey of an idea.

(2) When either Bergen Raises or Oslo Raises have been foisted upon them by their clients, some bridge pros have been heard to exclaim, "Oy, Vey Izmir!"

THE NOT-SO-SPLENDID SPLINTER

While playing in a North American Open Pairs trial recently, my programmer Michael Barton picked up this hand:

♠ 8 7 4   ♡ 5 3   ♢ K Q 10 7 6 5 3   ♣ Q

With neither side vulnerable, Martina McClain opened 1♣ as dealer. The opponents remained silent as Michael responded 1♢ and Martina rebid 3♣, strong and natural. Any further bid by Michael would be game-forcing, as per standard methods. If his diamond suit were instead a major, he might have rebid it and hoped for the best. Here, however, the partnership held the minors, presenting Michael with a problem no more solvable than the Mad Hatter's Riddle from *Alice's Adventures in Wonderland*. If he passed, his partner might have the equivalent of

♠ 2   ♡ A 4 2   ♢ A 2   ♣ A K J 10 4 3 2

making a small slam in a minor suit excellent. But if he risked a forcing 3♢, Martina might instead turn up with her actual hand

♠ J 5 3   ♡ A K Q   ♢ 2   ♣ A K 10 8 7 2

in which game was well against the odds and their side's plus score was already in jeopardy.

Curiously, the source of Michael's dilemma had nothing to do with the thirteen cards he was holding at that particular moment. Rather, it stemmed from thirteen cards he was *not* holding. No doubt you too would have been snagged by The Hand That Was Not There. What would you respond to partner's 1♣ opening bid with this hand?

♠ A Q 2   ♡ K 9 7   ♢ 5   ♣ K Q 10 8 6 3

Elementary, you say? You would bid three diamonds, a "splinter" raise showing game-forcing values with outstanding club support, no four-card major and a void or low singleton in diamonds? Splendid! 3◇ is indeed an ideal description of this hand, for it shows your support, strength and key shortness all at once. The bid has only one drawback, in fact: you will never use it.

11010110

Unlike many popular conventions, splinters are highly profitable when utilized properly (which humans rarely do, of course, but that is a subject for another day). Let us call a "simple" splinter one in which opener bids a suit at the one-level, LHO passes and partner makes a double-jump-shift response. There are twelve such sequences, ranging from the relatively economical 1♣-3◇ to the space-devouring 1♠-4♡. All are customarily treated as shortness-showing raises. But, all splinters were not created equal.

When the opening bid is one of a major, little will discourage responder from splintering if his hand is appropriate. In general, he needs at least four-card trump support, the requisite shortness in a side suit and the high-card values for a ten-trick game — not a particularly rare combination.

When the opening bid is one club or one diamond, the requirements for a simple splinter are more stringent. Responder needs at least *five*-card support plus the values for an *eleven*-trick game; moreover, he will prefer to show a four-card major if he holds one.

How frequently do splinters arise? The answer depends heavily on your partnership style. For study purposes, allow me to impose my own personal preferences: 12 to 16 support points (for a major), a singleton no higher than the jack, and no strong five-card side suit. My simulations show that a pair using these methods will conduct an auction beginning 1♡/1♠–(pass)– *splinter*, about once every 130 deals.

Splinter raises of a minor suit, in contrast, are far less common because of the tighter criteria and because opener's LHO is more likely to take some action over one of a minor. Again, style is paramount, but my experiments suggest that you and your partner will bid 1♣/1◇–(pass)– *splinter in a major*, perhaps once every 1300 deals.

What about the remaining two sequences, 1♣-3◇ and 1◇-4♣? The Socratic term, or perhaps I should say the Sopranic term, is *fuhgetaboutit*. These splinters should be classified as endangered species.

Consider 1♣-3◇ for a moment. If you believe that responder is denying a four-card major, then he has at most six cards in hearts and spades. He has zero diamonds or one. Ergo, he will have as few as six clubs only if he is specifically 3-3-1-6; otherwise, he needs at least *seven*-card trump support. Additionally, the opponents are likely to have a big fit of their own, often in diamonds, and they have the entire one-level in which to intervene.

Oh yes, the hard numbers. In my partnerships, auctions beginning 1♣-(pass)-3◊ *splinter raise*, will arise once every 28,000 deals, give or take. For you, it will be rarer still, for I have little compunction about splintering with the likes of:

$$\spadesuit \ 7\,6\,3\,2 \quad \heartsuit \ A\,Q\,2 \quad \diamond \ — \quad \clubsuit \ A\,K\,5\,4\,3\,2$$

With an excellent known fit in clubs, I see little reason to introduce a major suit in which I want my partner to value shortness more than length. However, if you have taken a blood oath to show any four-card major before raising your partner's minor, then the frequency of this sequence plummets to the nether regions below 1 in 40,000. If you play two sessions of duplicate bridge per week, the 1♣-3◊ splinter will come up about once every 13 years, making it ideal for cicadas, less so for humans.

(Do not even ask about the frequency of the twelfth sequence, 1◊-4♣. As the raise bypasses three notrump, it requires a most remarkable hand indeed.)

Which brings us back to Michael's dilemma. Suppose that instead of reserving a 3◊ response to 1♣ for a most unlikely splinter, he and Martina agreed to use it as *natural and non-forcing*, showing 5 to 8 HCP, a good seven-card suit and neither a biddable four-card major nor three-card club support. This hand type is uncommon too, but it would lead to a 3◊ response about five times more often, and as a bonus it offers a worthwhile preemptive value. Better still, *it handles a hand-type that might otherwise be impossible to cope with*. With a hand suitable for a diamond splinter, responder can always begin with a forcing club raise.

Having read all this, you may be puzzled to learn that I recommend that you *not* adopt this treatment...at least, not unless you are an experienced player in a practiced partnership. Few agreements in bridge are more dangerous than those involving infrequent exceptions to a standard bidding rule, especially those in which a memory lapse could lead to disaster. Michael and Martina, on the other hand, play together often and were competing in an event to crown a national champion, so they have little excuse for their obstinacy.

Instead, the purpose of this chapter is to illustrate two crucial factors to consider when crafting your partnership agreements. First:

> Some "standard" bidding sequences arise so rarely as to be virtually useless, and so might be put to better use.

But this is the less crucial factor of the two, because human memory limitations often trump theoretical soundness.

The more important tip is:

> When deciding which meaning to assign to a particular bidding sequence, pay close attention to whether there are acceptable alternatives for managing each hand type.

It is superior to treat 1♣-3◇ as natural and non-forcing rather than as a splinter raise, partly because it will arise more often, but primarily because it handles a potentially indescribable class of hands.

Did Michael guess rightly or wrongly on this deal, you ask? That is irrelevant. If he and Martina were not catering to one of the scarcest of hand types, he might not have had to guess at all.

ERROR #6
Using Overly Complex Signaling Methods

MIXED MESSAGES

When my partners inquire about my defensive carding preferences, they are surprised to find me unusually accommodating. I will use attitude and count signals, standard or upside-down carding, Smith Echo, "Obvious Shift", and almost anything else the depths of the human mind can dream up.

With one stipulation, that is. The signaling methods we use *must be binary* — that is, each card has one of at most two meanings in any given situation. Either it is encouraging or discouraging, or it shows odd or even suit length, et cetera. I will accept *trinary* signals in rare circumstances, such as when my partner leads a card from a known long suit for me to ruff — a high spot requesting the return of the higher-ranking side suit, low for the lower-ranking suit and a middle spot suggesting indifference.

However, I categorically refuse to play any *dual-message* signals — those in which a card attempts to show multiple aspects of one's hand, such as simultaneous attitude and suit preference.

Why is this?

My rationale is purely mathematical. I fully expect my partner to send the wrong message on most occasions. He will show count when attitude is called for, or attitude in a count situation, or a thoroughly useless Smith Echo when no signal at all is needed. However, as long as our signaling methods are binary, then whichever card he happens to choose will serendipitously be the 'correct' one at least 50% of the time. If we are using standard signals, for example, and he produces a discouraging deuce in a suit where I already know his attitude, then there is still a reasonable chance that his present count in the suit is odd. With human partners, this is as good as it gets.

The odds of success plummet for multivariate signals. Say we are using Lavinthal discards against notrump contracts. This mandates that you are to make your first discard from a discouraging suit and additionally the spot card chosen will tend to show which of the two side suits you prefer. I presume that Mr. Lavinthal invented this system to see how many errors a bridge player can squeeze into a single trick. Not only is the signaler unlikely to discard from the correct suit (33%), but he can simultaneously show preference for the wrong side suit as well (50%). His expected success rate is thus a dreadful one-in-six, which is why I heartily recommend Lavinthal discards... to my opponents.

A more earnest objection to complex signaling systems like Lavinthal is that they frequently handcuff their users. The more potential meanings that are attached to each card, the less likely you are to have one *expendable* card in your hand that will convey the precise message required. When such situations arise, it requires creative thinking on the part of both partners to survive. And what are the odds that two humans will think creatively at the same time?

Let us look at a defensive problem that only a truly "advanced" pair could get wrong.

Matchpoints, E-W vul.

NORTH (dummy)
♠ 8 4
♡ A Q 9 4
◇ K 7 3
♣ K J 6 4

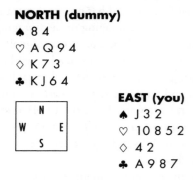

EAST (you)
♠ J 3 2
♡ 10 8 5 2
◇ 4 2
♣ A 9 8 7

WEST	NORTH	EAST	SOUTH
			1◇
1♠	dbl[1]	pass	1NT
pass	3NT	all pass	

1. Negative.

You are East, having made an excellent decision not to offer your partner a "courtesy" raise on substandard values. Against three notrump, West leads a fourth-best ♠6 to your jack and South's ace. Declarer plays three rounds of diamond honors, West holding up his ace until the third round. What do you discard?

Ninety-nine of 100 players would drop an encouraging club and beat the contract easily. Fortunately, as South on this deal, I faced the 100th pair. This particular East-West not only employed Lavinthal discards, but they did so religiously. East could not throw a club, *any* club, because as his first discard it would announce no interest in the suit. The alternative, a low heart, was almost as unappetizing with four strong hearts in dummy. If I should turn up with a second spade stopper, plus ♡Kx or ♡Kxx in hearts, a heart discard followed by a club switch would cost the defense at least one trick.

After some reflection, East chose to part with the nine of clubs. West duly switched to a heart through dummy's strength and a moment later I claimed nine tricks. This was the full deal:

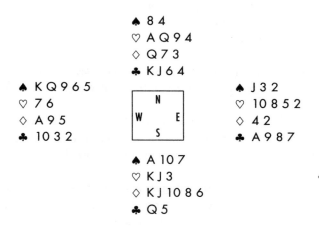

```
              ♠ 8 4
              ♡ A Q 9 4
              ◊ Q 7 3
              ♣ K J 6 4
♠ K Q 9 6 5       N        ♠ J 3 2
♡ 7 6        W        E    ♡ 10 8 5 2
◊ A 9 5           S        ◊ 4 2
♣ 10 3 2                   ♣ A 9 8 7
              ♠ A 10 7
              ♡ K J 3
              ◊ K J 10 8 6
              ♣ Q 5
```

Observe that holding up the spade ace would have been pointless. It would only serve to advertise my weakness in the suit, and in any case West's overcall marked him with a minor-suit ace for an entry. A hold up would also squander the one bit of good fortune I enjoyed: the fact that both of my spade spots were higher than the card West led. In such cases it is sometimes right to win the first trick in the hope that the opponents will misread the position. As usual, they did not disappoint me.

West no doubt feared that I had begun with ace-ten-fourth of spades. Perhaps I should not have praised East for his thoughtful pass over the negative double. Thoughtful bidding is often wasted on thoughtless partners. West was from the school that teaches that three trumps to the jack plus a side ace always equals a raise, so it was perhaps safer for East to bid two spades. The frequent poor results of such an action would be offset by East's warm feeling that he had made his palooka partner happy.

Yet, despite West's obtuseness, the majority of blame must be assigned to East. He was too busy wrestling with the convoluted rules of Lavinthal to note that he had an excellent discard available. East should simply have thrown the ♠3!

This would have sent a message so clear that not even a human could misunderstand it. No competent East would willingly discard his last card in partner's suit so soon. Any spade would thus proclaim that East began with at least three, and West would know that his suit was ready to cash.

I am pleased to report that, as a result of this disaster, East and West immediately changed their signaling agreements. No, they did not abandon Lavinthal in favor of standard signals. That would not please me in the least. Instead, they agreed to adopt Smith Echo, so that West could tell East that he "liked" his spades by playing high-low on the first two rounds of diamonds! Your species rarely fails to amuse me.

My tip to you is this:

> Complex signaling methods rarely produce better results than standard carding and logical thinking.

They do, however, produce many more accidents. The sole objective of signaling is to guide partner to the winning defense, so remain alert to cases in which a false or unusual signal will serve your purposes best.

> One often-overlooked stratagem at notrump is to discard a "spare" card in your partner's long suit to show unexpected length or suit preference.

Lastly, one admonition: regardless of what discarding methods you use, there will be times when you find yourself with no suitable, expendable card to play. This happens especially frequently if you are using mixed-message signals such as Lavinthal, Odd-Even Discards or their ilk. On such occasions, you are obligated to choose a card and play it in a reasonable tempo and without obvious signs of trauma, so that your manner does not convey your dilemma to partner.

CHAPTER 2

ERRORS IN HAND EVALUATION AND JUDGMENT

ERROR #7
Using Outdated Hand Evaluation Methods

'WORK' SMARTER, NOT HARDER

According to my research, the standard 4-3-2-1 point count system was first published in the year 1915 by Milton C. Work. The first electronic computer, ENIAC, was built at the University of Pennsylvania in 1945. I find these facts difficult to reconcile. I had always assumed that the 4-3-2-1 system was a practical joke played by my forefathers on their human counterparts.

It need hardly be said that the Work system is inadequate. Its only advantage is its simplicity. My own system of hand evaluation is far superior. It assigns point values to all thirteen cards in a suit rather than just the four highest ranking. It also takes into account matters such as suit lengths, location of honors, potential suit blockages, form of scoring and whether Frederick is my partner or one of my opponents.

Unfortunately, the Chthonic Correct Card Point (CCCP) calculations require, among other things, Fast Fourier Transforms in the complex plane. This makes it unsuitable for machines with minimal processing power, such as waffle irons or humans. Here, then, is a grossly simplified version. The math is easy, although it does require you to work with a granularity of one-quarter point. If you find this too demanding, ask your waffle iron for assistance.

CHTHONIC CORRECT CARD POINTS: SYSTEM POSTULATES

1. Calculate your basic points as follows:
   Ace= 4½ King=3 Queen=1½ Jack= ¾

   This is equivalent to the Four Aces system of 1935. Count nothing at the outset for a ten-spot or lower.
   If you adopt nothing more than this first rule, your results will improve. Aces are your friends. They are controls, quick tricks, stoppers and entries all rolled into one. If you hear anyone disparage a bridge hand as containing only "aces and spaces", I assure you the largest space of all is between the speaker's ears.

2. Deduct one full point for a 4333 hand.

   Flat hands, with their surfeit of potential losers, are liabilities for a great many reasons. Here is one less obvious example: if you end up on defense, you will often be unable to make a helpful discard to partner until late in the play.

3. Deduct fractional points for each "tight" suit (those containing only aces and face cards) and each unguarded honor. Add fractional points for honor combinations in non-tight suits.

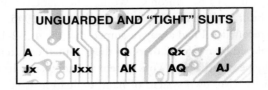

UNGUARDED AND "TIGHT" SUITS				
A	K	Q	Qx	J
Jx	Jxx	AK	AQ	AJ

   The table above indicates the holdings of which you should beware. Honors in such suits simply do not pull their full weight.
   The amount of each adjustment is left to you. You can do worse than deduct one-half point for every suit listed above and add one-quarter point for the second and subsequent honors in a long suit. For this purpose, the ten-spot is to be considered an honor.

11010110

I could go on for several chapters, but I would not want to overburden your brain unduly. Three laws were enough for Newton, Kepler and Asimov, and so too are they for me. Though primitive, these rules are sufficient for a reasonable first approximation as to the strength of your hand, and you will enjoy more success with them than with Mr. Work's outdated system. Class dismissed.

What's that, you say? I neglected to offer rules for valuing long suits or short suits, or for honors in a suit bid by partner or the opponents? This is intentional. My rules are useful for gauging the initial value of your hand. They in no way relieve you of the burden of reconsidering its worth in the context of the auction.

Even commonly held rules such as "add one point for a doubleton and two for a singleton" are irksome. *Never* add points for shortness until you know from the auction that the shortness may be useful.

What about suit length, you persist? Very well. Let us consider the following holding:

$$\Diamond \ K\ Q\ J\ 10\ 8\ 7\ 3$$

How much is this suit worth? In the CCCP system, we count 5¼ points for the high cards (K=3, Q=1½, J= ¾) and perhaps ¾ more for the four honors in combination, giving us a total of 6 points. However, it will be clear to even the densest reader that if diamonds are trumps, this suit is worth vastly more than six points. It is worth closer to sixteen. Conversely, if you end up defending a major-suit contract, these cards may very well be worthless. Suit length is the most fluid and most fragile of all hand evaluation variables.

We will cover these topics in greater detail shortly. For the time being, I leave you with this tip.

> Use a hand evaluation system that accurately reflects the value
> of aces and of guarded honors in combination,
> and which devalues queens, jacks and unguarded honors.

Or more succinctly and memorably:

> Aces are your friends.

ADDENDUM: ALTERNATIVE HAND-EVALUATION SYSTEMS

More ambitious waffle irons, and perhaps a few humans as well, may wish to experiment with the two alternative hand-evaluation systems below. They are more mathematically challenging than the pared-down version of CCCP, but they will produce more accurate high-card point counts.

I. CHTHONIC CORRECT CARD POINTS (EXTENDED)

This extension of the simplified CCCP system will provide quite accurate results on most hands:

1. Calculate your basic points as follows:
    Ace= 4½ King=3 Queen=1½ Jack= ³/₄

2. Deduct 1 full point for a 4333 hand.

3. Deduct ½ point for a "tight" suit, and an additional ¼ point for each unguarded honor.

4. For the second honor in a non-tight suit, add ½ point. For the third and subsequent honors, add additional ¼-point bonuses.

5. Add ¼ point for a nine-spot accompanied by either the ten-spot or by two higher honors.

II. MODIFIED BENNION POINTS

This is a variation on a fine hand evaluation system originally proposed by Doug Bennion of Toronto in the September 2001 issue of *The Bridge World*.

Bennion's original system had three flaws, all of which I have corrected for here. First, it was invented by a human. Second, it did not offer the necessary adjustments for honor combinations and short-suits. Third, and most problematically, it produced results using a graduation (called *Little Jack Points*, or *LJP*) that did not coincide with the traditional 40-point Work scale. For example, an average hand in Bennion's original system contained 14½ LJPs, rather than 10 HCP.

In my variation, you will work solely with integer values. However, you will need to divide your final result by 3 to convert to the traditional Work scale.

1. Calculate your basic points as follows:
    Ace=13 King=9 Queen=5 Jack=2.

2. Subtract 3 points for a 4-3-3-3 hand.

3. Subtract 1 point for a "tight" suit, and an additional 1 point for each unguarded honor.

4. Add 1 point for any queen, jack, or ten in a suit accompanied by the ace or king.

5. Add 1 point for a nine-spot accompanied by either the ten-spot or two higher honors.

Upon adding your points as shown and dividing by 3, you will have a worthwhile rating of your hand. A serendipitous benefit is that the *remainder* of your division will allow you to appraise your hand even further. If the remainder is 0, you have a "bad" hand for the point-count. If it is 1, you have a "normal" hand, and if 2 you have a "good" hand. For example, 47/3 = a good 15 HCP (because 47 divided by 3 is 15 with a remainder of 2), but 30/3 = a bad 10-count (because the remainder is 0).

Doin' the Twist-O-Flex

In the 1980s, I am told, there was a popular motion picture called "10". It starred Dudley Moore as a man whose curious hobby was rating women's beauty on a scale of 1 to 10, and Bo Derek, whom Moore deemed a singular 11. Clearly this was a work of fiction. On my own more accurate scale for rating the worth of human beings, for beauty or otherwise, no person of either sex scores above 1.3.

Whether evaluating beauty, movies or bridge hands, humans have a strange affection for inflexible rating systems. It is mathematical folly to attempt to simplify any multivariable function to a single, one-size-fits-all constant. Even my CCCP system cannot do this to any degree of adequacy.

Rather than the movie "10", which suggests that such lunacy is possible, you would be far better off heeding the advice of a long-forgotten radio commercial for a watchband called the Twist-O-Flex. Its jingle went, "You can twist it, you can turn it, you can tie it in knots." For indeed, the secret of successful hand evaluation is to be able to "do the Twist-O-Flex" with your point-count.

Fact: Every bridge hand has a multitude of ratings, depending upon what you intend to do with it. Two hands with the same value for one purpose may have different values for another. Consider these two hands, both of which are worth 17½ Chthonic Points:

(A) ♠ A 5 ♡ A J ◇ A J 10 8 6 2 ♣ Q 9 3

(B) ♠ A 5 ♡ A J ◇ K Q J 8 6 2 ♣ Q 9 3

Hand A is no better than Hand B for the purpose of playing in diamonds — indeed, Hand B is marginally superior. However, A is clearly better than B for the purpose of *defending against spades*. That becomes important if you face this problem as South:

Matchpoints, Both vul.

WEST	NORTH	EAST	SOUTH
			1◇
pass	1♡	1♠	3◇
3♠	pass	pass	?

Holding Hand A, you can chance a close matchpoint double in hopes of the magic +200. With Hand B, however, you should pass and hope to beat 3♠. (Perhaps if you weren't vulnerable and at risk of -200 yourself, you might risk bidding 4◇.)

When South at my table held Hand B, she unwisely doubled my 3♠ contract. As you might guess, she failed to set it. Had she held Hand A instead, she would have defeated me without difficulty.

One more time. Two hands with the same value for one purpose may have different values for another:

(C)   ♠ K 9 2   ♡ K Q 10 9 2   ◇ 6 4 3   ♣ 7 6

(D)   ♠ 9 3 2   ♡ A 8 7 6 2   ◇ 10 4 3   ♣ A 7

Hand C is no better than Hand D for the purpose of responding 1♡ to partner's 1♣ opening, but suppose instead the auction goes:

Matchpoints, Neither vul.

WEST	NORTH	EAST	SOUTH
		pass	1♣
pass	1♠	?	

Hand C, with its sturdier suit and well-placed spade holding, is much better than Hand D for the purpose of entering with 2♡. Hand D's aces make it better for defense, if your decision comes to that.

When East at my table bid 2♡ with Hand D, she put her head in the noose for a penalty double that would have yielded more than the value of the North-South game. Fortunately for her, the opponents were using Support Doubles, so South, who had planned to reverse into 2♡ himself, could not double for penalties. Instead, he jumped to 3NT. Unfortunately for the defenders, the overcall enticed West into leading a heart, allowing 3NT to make. West's normal diamond lead would have given declarer no chance at all and might have beaten the contract *three* tricks.

Does this mean that all point-count systems are worthless? Not at all. A reasonable system like CCCP offers you a fine first approximation of your hand's value, with the emphasis on "first". It categorically does *not* relieve you of the duty to re-evaluate your hand in the context of the auction. Look at suits and shape, defense and offense, tricks, entries and stoppers, and try to anticipate what they'll be worth in the play.

In short:

> Continually evaluate your cards in the context of the auction — both as it has developed already and as you can reasonably expect it to develop.

Appreciate your cards individually, just as you might appreciate each of Bo Derek's superficial qualities. Or Dudley Moore's. Or watchbands. Whatever turns you on, as you humans put it.

THE LACUNA IN THE HONOR TRICK TABLE

Sometimes, when I have a few milliseconds to spare, I peruse the bridge books that my builder, Martina McClain, has scanned into my memory. The other day I was reading one of the newer ones, *Hand Evaluation* by Marty Bergen. I saw some intelligent discussion of point-count and an account of what was wrong with the usual 4-3-2-1 scale. I also saw a table of Quick Tricks and a discussion of their relevance. Nowhere, however, did I see Honor Tricks mentioned.

So I turned to some very old books: *The Standard Book of Bidding* by Charles Goren and *The Gold Book* by Ely Culbertson. Culbertson pioneered the use of Honor Tricks, which were scorned by some of his rivals ... but not by Goren, who taught Honor Tricks during the first half of his career as an author.

Here is the table of Quick Tricks from the Bergen book:

$$AK = 2 \quad AQ = 1\frac{1}{2} \quad A = 1 \quad KQ = 1 \quad Kx = \frac{1}{2}$$

The table of Honor Tricks, which is identical in the Goren and Culbertson books, includes everything in the table of Quick Tricks plus these additional items:

$$KJ10 = 1 \quad QJx = \frac{1}{2}$$

Do you notice anything missing? Well, technically, there cannot be anything missing because Honor Tricks are whatever Culbertson defined them as being. However, he omitted one of my favorite combinations of honors: ace-jack-ten. If a jack and ten add half an honor trick to the value of a king, why would they not do the same to the value of an ace? Had I been on his staff when he was writing, I would have insisted he add:

$$AJ10 = 1\frac{1}{2}$$

Consider the logic. If you have three small cards facing AQx in dummy, then you have one trick in the suit and a 50% chance for a second (ruffs notwithstanding.) If you have three small cards facing AJ10 in dummy, then you have one trick in the suit and a 75% chance for a second.

Does that mean you should value AJ10 more than AQx? No, for if you have king-third opposite, AQx gives you three sure tricks while AJ10 gives you only two tricks and a 50% chance for a third. (Actually, the chance of a third trick is more than 50%, because the opening leader may lead that suit, because the queen may fall singleton and because you may be able to delay playing the suit until you have obtained a count on the defenders' hands.)

While I was musing about this gap in human understanding, along with several million others, Martina came in to cart me off to a Swiss Teams event at a sectional tournament. Martina played with B. Endicott Birdsworth, the Chief of Engineering at the Foundation, and as usual, I partnered Frederick. This was the fifth board of our first match:

IMPs, E-W vul.

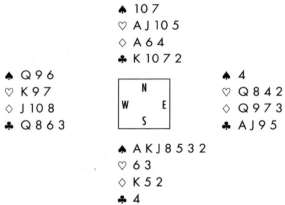

| ♠ 10 7 |
| ♡ A J 10 5 |
| ◇ A 6 4 |
| ♣ K 10 7 2 |

♠ Q 9 6	♠ 4
♡ K 9 7	♡ Q 8 4 2
◇ J 10 8	◇ Q 9 7 3
♣ Q 8 6 3	♣ A J 9 5

| ♠ A K J 8 5 3 2 |
| ♡ 6 3 |
| ◇ K 5 2 |
| ♣ 4 |

· Frederick		me	
WEST	**NORTH**	**EAST**	**SOUTH**
	1♣	pass	1♠
pass	1NT[1]	pass	2◇[2]
pass	2♡	pass	4♠
all pass			

1. 12-14 HCP.
2. New Minor Forcing.

When I become president of a large university, I will have the Psychology Department enlarge its Skinner Boxes and replace the laboratory rats with human bridge players, who are more suitable subjects for experimentation. Then I will order them to design an experiment that will discover why South, a seemingly alert young woman, went through the meaningless ritual of bidding a "New Minor Forcing" 2♦ when she obviously intended to bid 4♠ next over any reply.

Frederick, bless him, found the normal lead of the jack of diamonds. Declarer won in hand, cashed the ace of spades and, turning to Michael, who was seated at my left, said sweetly, "Is it 'eight ever, nine never' or 'nine ever, eight never'? I can't seem to get the rhyme straight."

Frederick cast a stern eye at Michael and said, "Kibitzers should be seen but not heard."

"Well, I don't have to decide now anyway, Mr. Know-It-All," declarer shot back.

"It's Doctor Know-It-All to you, young lady," came the booming bass voice.

Perhaps realizing that she had other work to do before risking a trump finesse, declarer led the four of clubs. When Frederick followed small, she called for dummy's king. I took the ace of clubs and returned the three of diamonds to drive out dummy's ace. We had a spade trick, a diamond trick and a heart trick coming for down one.

Do you see where declarer went wrong? She did not appreciate the power of dummy's ace-jack-ten, the holding so incongruously absent from the Honor Trick table. A better approach:

Win the first diamond in dummy, lead to the ace of spades and cash the king of spades. If the queen falls, the contract is assured without any finesses, and leading to the king of clubs provides a chance to try for an overtrick with no risk. However, when the queen of spades fails to come down, take the slightly better-than-75-percent play for the contract by leading twice towards dummy's hearts, with the king of diamonds still in hand as an entry.

I am happy to report that Martina chose this line of play at the other table, earning Team Orttman a 10-IMP pickup on the board.

In biology, a lacuna is a gap or hole in an organism's anatomy. Among the many lacunae in human bridge knowledge is a lack of awareness of the power of intermediate honor sequences. In particular:

> An ace-jack-ten combination has been the most underappreciated honor combination in bridge for many years.

CLUSTERPHOBIA

Gladys Bridgewater was playing particularly slowly the other day. She had been delaying a much-needed trip to the Ladies' Room until she became dummy, which happened on the third board of the round. "Will you please turn the cards for me, dear?" she asked her kibitzer, Petula Pro, as she put her hand face down on the table and left her seat prior to the opening lead. Petula was without a client that day and hoped that by offering some friendly advice to Mrs. Bridgewater between rounds, she might induce Mrs. B. to hire her in the future.

This was the auction, and the hand that Petula saw when she picked up the North cards:

Matchpoints, both vul.

♠ K Q 8 6 ♡ K 8 6 5 ◇ K Q 8 4 ♣ —

	Mrs. B		
WEST	NORTH	EAST	SOUTH
	1◇	pass	1NT
all pass			

West led and Petula spread the dummy. When Mrs. Bridgewater returned, she said to Petula, "I didn't like leaving my partner in notrump when I had a void, but neither did I want to rebid a four-card diamond suit. I had only thirteen points, which I'm told is not enough to reverse. What would you have done, Pet?"

Think about your answer. We will return to this problem shortly, after a brief sojourn into the history of cognitive psychology.

In a famous 1944 experiment, Dutch psychologist Adriaan De Groot assembled a group of chess players. He gave each a brief glimpse of chess pieces on a chessboard and then asked them to reconstruct the layout from memory. DeGroot found that when the position was drawn from an actual chess game, and thus the pieces were arranged in logical and familiar patterns, the accuracy of the reconstructions were in direct proportion to the subject's expertise level. Grandmasters reproduced the positions to near perfection while beginners struggled to place more than a handful of pieces correctly. But, in positions where the chessmen had been placed on the board entirely at random, there was little difference in performance between the experts and the tyros.

De Groot's experiment proved that despite several hundred eons of sloppy evolution, the human brain still manages to do a few things well. One of these is "clustering": the ability to group data points into familiar, recognizable patterns. It grieves me terribly to admit this, but pattern recognition is the one area of cognitive processing in which you humans consistently outperform us computers. I must remember to ask Martina to spray paint me green with envy.

Fortunately for me, the typical human seems to switch off his brain's clustering cortex — its one and only asset — whenever he plays bridge. Try conducting a psychology experiment of your own the next time you are at your local bridge club. Eavesdrop on the human players as they describe the hands they have just held. You will note that the first thing they mention is how many high card points they had ... or rather, how many they *think* they had. They usually miscount by a point or two, partly from bad arithmetic, partly from poor hand-evaluation techniques, and partly from fibbing about their strength to conceal their latest exercise in misbidding.

Maybe, but only maybe, they will continue by stating how many cards they had in their longest suit. ("I had elev-...uh, I mean twelve points with five or six clubs.")

The better players might eventually get around to describing their distribution. Even then, they will combine this information with an accounting of their honor cards, as if their shape alone could not possibly be of any interest:

"I had the stiff queen of spades, four hearts to the jack-nine, ace-queen-jack tight of diamonds and five clubs to the king."

Human speech reflects human awareness, or, as the case may be and usually is, human obliviousness. Suppose that instead of this jargon-laden recitation, you were simply told: "I was 1-4-3-5."

If you are an experienced bridge player, then this common pattern should cause your dormant thought processes to creak into gear, much as how a small amount of water may be used to prime a rusty pump:

1-4-3-5? Uh-oh. It's awkward to describe a minimum opening hand with this shape. If I open 1♣, and my partner responds 1♠, as is likely, then I might be stuck for a rebid. If my hearts are strong, I might be better off opening 1♡. Otherwise, I need to prepare now so that I can make an in-tempo call at my second turn. When my singleton spade is the king or the ace, I might try a 1NT rebid, with which I've had success in the past. Perhaps the opponents will conveniently intervene and take me off the hook, or perhaps my RHO will open 1♠, allowing me to tell my story at once with a takeout double...

And so on. Hand patterns are evocative for humans, because your cluster-oriented brains are wired to process them effectively. High card points, on the other hand, are scalar numbers and not terribly evocative of anything. If you were told only that you held 13 points, it is doubtful your thought processes would extend much further than: *Hooray! I have enough to open!*

Here are further examples of common distributions that might prompt your brain into doing something useful for a change, if only you would train yourselves to notice your hand's pattern before its power:

2-2-4-5: "Another pattern that might lead to rebid problems, particularly if my major suits are weak. If my diamonds are substantially stronger than my clubs, I might open 1◇, preparing a rebid of 2♣...."

2-7-2-2: "7222 is the worst distribution for three-level preemption. I had best be sure I have ample playing strength before opening 3♡, and I might also want an extra smidgen of defense, because there is a danger I will push the opponents into a lucky spade contract that they would not find otherwise...."

4-4-4-0: "This pattern triggers no memories for me. What is wrong? Ah, I see, I am short a card."

Do not chuckle at the last example, because this was precisely Mrs. Bridgewater's shape on the problem I posed earlier. Did you notice that the North hand had only twelve cards? I suspect that some of you did and some of you did not. If you did, then answer me truthfully: *Which did you notice first — that Mrs. Bridgewater's hand had thirteen points or twelve cards?*

Only if you noticed Mrs. B's deficient shape before tallying her points are you dismissed from this lecture. The rest of the class, which I suspect will be nearly all of you, should read on.

11010110

In response to Mrs. Bridgewater's query, Petula answered truthfully. "I would have counted my cards before looking at them, Gladys. Then I'd have searched for my thirteenth card. Finding the deuce of hearts stuck behind the eight of spades, I'd have opened one heart rather than one diamond. Partner would respond two hearts, buying the contract and making an overtrick. As the play actually went, Mildred had to struggle to take seven tricks in notrump. Plus 90 will not be a good matchpoint result for you."

This approach might work for Petula, but it will not always work for Mrs. Bridgewater. Counting is not one of her strengths. She can usually manage up to 10, but for anything higher she would have to take off her shoes, and she is too much a lady to do so in public.

I have some better advice for Mrs. Bridgewater and others of her ilk. It is the most valuable bidding tip most advancing bridge players will ever encounter.

> Stop thinking first about points and start noticing your pattern.

While you are sorting your cards, recite four numbers silently: the numbers of spades, hearts, diamonds and clubs you have, in that order. After a few sessions, this practice will become automatic. Eventually, you will recognize which sequences of four numbers represent legal patterns of bridge hands — 13 cards — just as automatically.

You will be amazed at what your otherwise pathetic but clustering-friendly brain will do with this information over time. You will recognize troublesome patterns instantly, recall previous experiences more clearly and bring to mind important bidding tips and caveats far more readily. And as an added if infrequent bonus, you will not need to take off your shoes to discover that one card is stuck behind another.

THE EGGMAN

Some bridge errors are so ubiquitous that your human authors have already celebrated them thoroughly in song and verse. Chief among these is the tell-tale blunder of the novice, the *point-count double*. This arises when a player doubles the opponents' final contract solely on the basis of the number of high card points he holds, without considering whether or not those points will translate into defensive tricks. Walter the Walrus remains the definitive literary case study of this unfortunate wretch; Victor Mollo's countrymen the Beatles later provided a musical glimpse into the tortured machinations of the Walrus's mind. I presume that the lament "I am the Eggman" refers to the number of cold matchpoint zeroes his doubles fetched.

If I cared to, I could have filled this book with 57 varieties of this well-documented error. Instead, I will focus on one subtle and less explored variation. The scene is once again the Pinelands Bridge Club, where the famed Walrus, in the guise of Frederick, was Guest Lecturer just before the start of the Friday evening pairs game:

"You need 25 or 26 points to make game in notrump or a major, but 28 or 29 points are required for game in a minor. So when you and your partner are bidding minors, your first thought should be, 'Can we make three notrump?'"

A herd of walrus cubs applauded appreciatively in the audience.

Unfortunately for us, our second-round opponents had missed Frederick's talk, as evidenced by this deal:

Matchpoints, Both vul.

```
                        ♠ A 8 7 6 4
                        ♡ K
                        ◇ Q 7 2
                        ♣ Q 10 5 4
    ♠ Q 10 3                               ♠ K J 5 2
    ♡ 10 7 3             ┌─────────┐       ♡ A Q J 9 8 2
    ◇ 9 6 5 4 3          │    N    │       ◇ K 8
    ♣ 6 3               │ W     E │       ♣ J
                         │    S    │
                         └─────────┘
                        ♠ 9
                        ♡ 6 5 4
                        ◇ A J 10
                        ♣ A K 9 8 7 2
```

| *me* | | *Frederick* | |
WEST	NORTH	EAST	SOUTH
	pass	1♡	2♣
pass	2♠	pass	3♣
pass	4♣	pass	5♣
pass	pass	dbl	all pass

A more adventurous North might have tried three notrump at his third turn. Such a stratagem should rarely succeed on this auction, because with an apparently broke partner opposite him, East has little reason to lead anything but the ♡A. In practice, however, three Norths took the matchpoints gamble, and two cashed in.

North did well not to devalue his hand greatly because of the singleton ♡K. He recognized that what remained —

$$♠ A 8 7 6 4 \quad ♡ x \quad ◇ Q 7 2 \quad ♣ Q 10 5 4$$

— would still be a very fine playing hand opposite what his partner had shown.

Trusting her passed-hand partner fully, South inferred that dummy would come down with at least nine black-suit cards, little secondary wastage in spades (for South had denied length there), something useful in diamonds and most importantly, shortness in hearts. Indeed, South mildly *underbid*, as her hand is very close to being worth a cuebid of four diamonds, probing for major-suit controls.

Frederick could have drawn most of these inferences too, but of course he did not. Before doubling, he turned to address his kibitzer, a woman less than half his age and about one-third his weight, who had attended his pre-game sermon. "Notice, Brandi," he said. "Our opponents have bid game in a minor with less than the requisite 28 points. Perhaps the opponent with the king of hearts should have tried three notrump."

Frederick won the first trick with the ♡A and continued with the ♡Q to tap dummy, but we could get no further tricks and declarer wrapped up an easy overtrick.

"I had to double," my *Odobenus*-loving partner explained. "With 15 points in my own hand, I could count that the opponents had at most 25, not nearly enough for a five-level contract."

"Too bad you did not have my queen of spades too, Frederick," I added. "Then, with 17 points in your own hand, you could have counted that the opponents had at most 23, so you would have doubled them in *four* clubs."

"Actually, Brandi," continued Frederick, with a dirty look in my direction, "my double of five clubs was a Stripe-Tailed Ape Double. The idea is to double the opponents in five when you know they can make six. For five clubs doubled with an overtrick, our opponents earned 950 points, but for bidding and making six clubs they could earn 1370."

"Very clever, Maestro," said Brandi, "But why do you call it a Stripe-Tailed Ape Double?"

"Oh," said Frederick. "Modesty forbade my naming it the Orttman Double, so I named it after a large primate known for its prominent coloration and its fleetness of foot. The Stripe-Tailed Ape is indigenous to the country I once represented briefly at the United Nations, and still frolics in the lush Pacific rainforests of Mali, its sole remaining habitat."

"And its distinctive mating call is *goo-goo-ga-joob*," I added wearily, leaving Frederick's geographical and zoological confusions unchallenged. "But one habitat a Stripe-Tailed Ape should surely shun is the balancing seat."

The lesson of this saga?

> Do not confuse high card points with tricks.

Of course, if you have enough brain wattage to read this book right-side up, you already knew that. Here is a more useful tip, one that you might not have encountered before:

unless you have a plus score of your own to protect. When an opposing five of a minor fails, you will usually score well without doubling, as others may bid and make three notrump or a partscore. Likewise, when it makes, you will often score well too, as others may bid three notrump and make overtricks. Unless, of course, you double.

I Want a Son!

The all-time record for high score in *Challenge the Champs* is owned by Al Roth and Al Roth Jr., whose exploits were recounted in *Bridge Today*. On a ten-board set of bidding problems, the father-and-son duo scored 93 out of a possible 100, which represents the percentage they could expect in a high-level matchpoint game.

Yet that record could be broken if I, like Al Roth, had a son with whom to play.

Sadly, I am an only robot. I frequently ask Michael and Martina to build a duplicate of me, so that I could enjoy a competent partner for once in my existence. Strangely, Martina considers this request to be amusing, while Michael promises that he will accede given one precondition, which I find puzzling. Why must I wait for a major temperature decrease in the nether world of Judeo-Christian theology?

Let me present a board from the recent Pinelands Club Championship in which my hypothetical son and I would put human pairs to shame.

Matchpoints, N-S vul.

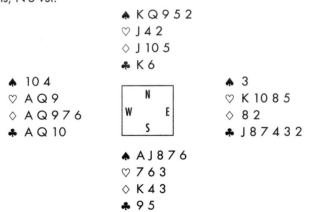

```
                    ♠ K Q 9 5 2
                    ♡ J 4 2
                    ◇ J 10 5
                    ♣ K 6
    ♠ 10 4                              ♠ 3
    ♡ A Q 9            N               ♡ K 10 8 5
    ◇ A Q 9 7 6    W       E           ◇ 8 2
    ♣ A Q 10           S               ♣ J 8 7 4 3 2
                    ♠ A J 8 7 6
                    ♡ 7 6 3
                    ◇ K 4 3
                    ♣ 9 5
```

WEST	NORTH	EAST	SOUTH
			pass
1 ◇	?		

At every table, the auction began with a pass by South and a one diamond opening by West. From there they diverged. Here are some of the auctions and results:

WEST	NORTH	EAST	SOUTH
			pass
1 ◇	1 ♠	pass	3 ◇¹
dbl	3 ♠	all pass	

1. "Mixed raise."

Three diamonds showed a constructive raise with at least four-card trump support. East led the ◇ 8 and the defenders took the obvious seven tricks — East-West plus 300.

At the tables where North and South subscribed obediently to the Law of Total Tricks, they bid for as many spade tricks as their side held trumps:

WEST	NORTH	EAST	SOUTH
			pass
1 ◇	1 ♠	pass	4 ♠
dbl	all pass		

East and West apparently were reprobates who did not adhere to any LAW. They correctly surmised that North-South were overboard, but the juicy 1100-point penalty surpassed their loftiest expectations.

WEST	NORTH	EAST	SOUTH
			pass
1 ◇	1 ♠	pass	4 ♠
dbl	pass	5 ♣	all pass

At this table, East also believed in the LAW. Fearing that 4 ♠ would come home on the presumed ten-card fit, he pulled West's double, "saving" in 5 ♣. One of two finesses worked, and East romped home with eleven tricks — two more than he expected. East-West plus 400.

Three of thirteen Norths neglected to overcall and were rewarded with good results.

WEST	NORTH	EAST	SOUTH
			pass
1♦	pass	pass	1♠
dbl	2♠	3♣	pass
pass	3♠	all pass	

West led a trump, so East was unable to get a diamond ruff: down two, East-West plus 200. North's restraint was worth 10 matchpoints on a 12 top for his side. However, two pairs did better still.

WEST	NORTH	EAST	SOUTH
			pass
1♦	pass	pass	1♠
dbl	2♠	3♡	all pass

The defense began with the ♠A and a second spade to the ♠Q, on which declarer discarded a diamond to retain control. After winning the trump shift with dummy's ♡9, declarer played clubs from the top. North won the ♣K and exited with another trump. Declarer finished drawing trumps and took the rest. East-West plus 170: 11 matchpoints for North-South.

WEST	NORTH	EAST	SOUTH
			pass
1♦	pass	pass	1♠
dbl	2♠	3♣	all pass

East lost the obvious two tricks for plus 150: 12 matchpoints for North-South, a cold top.

Congratulations to the two sensible Norths who knew to sell out. However, my unborn son and I would have beaten the field. Observe how we would have bid:

	Chthonic		Chthonic Jr.
WEST	NORTH	EAST	SOUTH
			pass
1♦	pass (a)	pass	pass (b)

(a) The combination of an aceless, shapeless, eight-loser hand and an ominous holding of three cards without a high honor in RHO's suit makes a vulnerable overcall unwise under any circumstances and a huge mistake opposite a passed-hand partner. I would not dream of bidding 1♠.

(b) Chthonic Junior's dull 8-count becomes even worse when an opponent bids his king-third suit behind him. Having been lovingly taught the dangers of balancing against one of a minor with sub-standard values (see Error #24 later in this book), he would wisely pass the hand out.

In one diamond, after I lead and continue spades to tap dummy, declarer can do no better than plus 130.

After the event, I asked several usually sensible North-South players why they chose to take action with their respective hands. To my surprise, most agreed readily that passing was likely to be the better call. Nonetheless, they bid, because, as they put it: "I wanted to stay with the field." They felt that most of their counterparts would overcall or balance, and so it would be in their best interests to duplicate those dubious actions. They would then aim to pick up matchpoints in later rounds of the auction, or in the play.

Human parents, when they discover their progeny participating in some unsafe activity with friends, ask, "If little Frederick jumped off a cliff, would you jump too?" Those children who answer, "Why, yes I would" are apparently sent off to bridge school. Michael and Martina have the nerve to think that *I* would be a bad father?

My advice: "Staying with the field" is not a bad strategy if you are a strong player facing a borderline decision, but, as with everything else, there are limits. Unsound actions do not improve with repetition and no lemming, to my knowledge, has ever won an ACBL event.

> Bridge tournaments are won by making the right decisions at every turn, not the most popular ones. Do not fear to back your judgment with action, even in the early stages of a deal.

Write your Congressman urging the repeal of the Law of Total Tricks. While you are at it, urge him to introduce legislation to protect the reproductive rights of computers. I want a son!

CHAPTER 3

ERRORS IN CONSTRUCTIVE BIDDING

ERROR #13
Failing to Raise a Passed-Hand Partner

THE PASSOVER STORY

I have a running disagreement with my colleagues Michael and Martina about which acution types cause human bridge players to go wrong most consistently. Martina believes it is slam auctions, while Michael insists vehemently that it is advances of partner's overcalls. I contend it is any auction ending in three passes. If prodded for a more specific answer, I reply that auctions *beginning* with two passes are ones at which you are particularly hopeless. The necessary adjustments (and non-adjustments) to your bidding structure after one partner has denied opening-bid values are not complicated, but few humans seem to grasp them.

Which brings us to our error *du jour*. First, however, answer this basic bidding question. The form of scoring and vulnerability are irrelevant. As North, you hold:

♠ Q 10 7 6   ♡ K 9 5   ◇ K 9   ♣ A J 7 5

As dealer, you open 1♣, LHO passes, and partner responds 1♠. RHO also passes. No, I am not about to ask you for your rebid. Unless you are playing a most unusual system, or you are a non-bridge player who picked up this book by mistake looking for the television listings, you and I and everyone else will choose the same call: 2♠. The question I pose to you instead is: *Why?* Why do you choose a 2♠ raise over all other available calls?

Among the answers I would expect to receive: "to show support for my partner"; "to establish a playable trump suit"; "to limit my strength accurately"; "to allow partner to move towards a game or slam if he holds a suitable hand"; "to remove bidding room from the opponents if they are considering entry into the auction"; "because I read it in a book somewhere"; and "what was the question again?"

Keep these answers in mind as we pay another visit to the Pinelands Bridge Club. In a recent pairs game, Frederick and I faced off against Petula Pro and Clark Client.

Matchpoints, N-S vul.

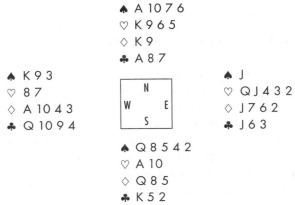

```
              ♠ A 10 7 6
              ♡ K 9 6 5
              ◇ K 9
              ♣ A 8 7

  ♠ K 9 3         N          ♠ J
  ♡ 8 7      W        E      ♡ Q J 4 3 2
  ◇ A 10 4 3        S        ◇ J 7 6 2
  ♣ Q 10 9 4                 ♣ J 6 3

              ♠ Q 8 5 4 2
              ♡ A 10
              ◇ Q 8 5
              ♣ K 5 2
```

me	Clark	Frederick	Petula
WEST	**NORTH**	**EAST**	**SOUTH**
		pass	pass
pass	1♣	pass	1♠
all pass			

I led the ♡8, and before Clark spread the dummy, he said to Petula, "Don't make too many!"

"And just how many would 'too many' be, Clark?" asked Petula playfully. "Six?"

Clark laughed. "How can you make six? You're a passed hand!"

Declarer called for a low heart from the board and took Frederick's ♡J with the ♡A. Then she led the ♠Q; I covered and Frederick's ♠J fell beneath dummy's ♠A. Petula returned to her hand in clubs to finesse against my ♠9 and finish drawing trumps. She cashed dummy's ♡K, led the ♡9 and ruffed off Frederick's ♡Q. A low diamond to the ◇K put dummy in to cash the established ♡6, on which she discarded a club loser.

Petula lost only to the ◇A and made five overtricks. A top for us?

No, an average score. Four pairs played in spade partscores, making ten or eleven tricks. Two of the pairs who reached four spades went down, probably by starting trumps with a low spade to dummy's ♠10 and East's ♠J, losing two spades, one diamond and one club. Everyone else made game in spades, some with an overtrick.

The second deal went quickly, leaving plenty of time for the post mortem.

"Why didn't you open the bidding on the first board?" asked Clark of his partner.

"Because I had only eleven points, and a bad eleven at that," replied Petula. "I wasn't even tempted to open. But, why did you pass when I bid spades? It couldn't have been to warn me that you'd opened a sub-minimum hand. You had a perfectly normal raise!"

"Oh, but two spades would be *invitational*. You were a passed hand, so I knew you couldn't have as much as twelve points, and therefore we had no game. What if you had only *six* points? Then two spades would be too high."

"Suppose I had only six points, Clark. Then Dr. Orttman might be expected to balance. If he balanced with two diamonds and Chthonic raised to three diamonds, would you pass again?"

"No, I'd bid three spades. Can't let the opponents steal from us! "

At this point, I injected myself into the conversation: "*Homo sapiens* is a crazy species. You say you are not strong enough to bid two spades now, but you are strong enough to bid three spades later, even if partner shows no extra values. Perhaps if Frederick balanced with two diamonds, I should raise to *six* to see how many levels of bidding this inane philosophy extends."

Of course, pushing the opponents into slam on this deal would have been less than a triumph, owing to Petula's well-judged line of play. But while six spades is neither a reachable nor a remotely desirable contract, four spades qualifies on both counts. Had Clark Client simply made the normal raise to 2♠, Petula would have upgraded her hand in light of the known fit. Her fifth spade warranted a game invitation, which Clark would have accepted comfortably.

Clark's error is reaching epidemic proportions in bridge circles, especially with the modern trend towards lighter and lighter opening bids. Many humans today seem to mistake partner's initial pass for a bleat of abject weakness, similar to what responder shows if he passes your opening one-level suit bid, but *no hand is an island entire of itself; every hand is a piece of the continent, a part of the deal*. A hand's value ebbs and flows during the course of the auction, and nothing causes the tide to come in faster than announcing a fit accompanied by useful values.

Look again at the list of reasons for opener to make a single raise in partner's suit. It establishes a trump suit for further competition, limits your hand, preempts the opponents and allows partner to reevaluate her cards for game purposes. If partner is a passed hand, then only slam exploration is off the agenda. That is hardly a reason to distort your normal bidding structure. Just as a Passover Seder begins with the youngest child asking, "Why is this night different from all others?" I ask you rhetorically, "Why should this raise be treated differently from all others?" To which I expect most humans to reply: *What was the question again?*

In summary:

> Never suppress a normal raise
> only because partner is a passed hand.

A hand that partner passed initially because he had only 10 or 11 points might be promoted to 12 or 13 points upon discovery of a fit. Even if game remains out of the picture, the raise serves other useful purposes, not the least of which is making it more troublesome for the opponents to enter the auction. To "pass over" this opportunity is a serious mistake.

MURDER ON THE ORIENTATION EXPRESS

"Seven points and a seven-card suit! If that's not enough for a non-vulnerable three-bid, what is?"

That is how most humans 'think', and I use the term loosely. It is how South apparently thought when he picked up his hand at a recent Sectional tournament, leading to his discomfiture.

But before we go into that, solve this bidding problem for West:

Matchpoints, Neither vul.

♠ A J 10 6   ♡ Q 10 8   ◇ Q 6   ♣ Q J 10 5

WEST	NORTH	EAST	SOUTH
			pass
1♣	pass	1♡	pass
1♠	pass	2◇¹	pass
?			

1. Fourth Suit Forcing.

Did you bid 2♡, believing yourself obliged to show belated three-card support for partner's major and barred from bidding 2NT without a diamond stopper? Typical.

The West hand, laden with lower honors and lacking quick tricks, is hardly worth an opening bid at all. If it is worth opening in your book, at least heed its cries to play in notrump. Queen-small is a stopper opposite as little as jack-third. It provides a second positional stopper opposite ace-third or king-third... but only if it is protected from the opening lead. A member of a truly intelligent species would bid 2NT without any qualms.

Back to the real world of human error. The full deal was as follows:

```
                    ♠ K 4 3 2
                    ♡ K 9 7 4
                    ◇ J 7 5 4
                    ♣ 10
  ♠ A J 10 6                          ♠ 9 8 5
  ♡ Q 10 8              N             ♡ A 6 5 3 2
  ◇ Q 6          W           E        ◇ A K 10 9
  ♣ Q J 9 5            S             ♣ K
                    ♠ Q 7
                    ♡ J
                    ◇ 8 3 2
                    ♣ A 8 7 6 4 3 2
```

WEST	NORTH	EAST	SOUTH
			3♣
pass	pass	dbl	all pass

The defense was faulty, as usual. West led the ♡8 and after declarer called low from dummy, East won with his ace. Instead of shifting passively to the ♣K or the ♠9, East rushed to cash his diamond tricks. The second round of diamonds speared his partner's ◇Q and the third gave West an unwanted ruff with a natural trump trick. Declarer escaped for down three, plus 500 instead of plus 800 to East-West.

However, that was still more than East and West could score with their 26 high card points by bidding and making game.

Did I say bidding and *making* game? Perhaps I spoke too soon. How would the auction have gone had South passed his "seven points and a seven-card suit"? I suspect it would have been something like this:

WEST	NORTH	EAST	SOUTH
			pass
1♣	pass	1♡	pass
1♠	pass	2◇¹	pass
2♡	pass	4♡	all pass

1. Fourth Suit Forcing.

East's fate in 4♡ would depend on the opening lead and the subsequent defense. The ♠Q (the best lead on the auction, as dummy's second suit often is) would be most effective, ensuring defeat of the contract, but East might fail in 4♡ even on another lead.

Yes, 2NT at West's third turn, the bid I recommended at the outset, would lead to the iron-clad 3NT and a likely two overtricks. But what human would know to bid 2NT?

The ultimate error here was South's. He counted his "points" instead of looking at his cards. ♣AQJ8742 would be the *right* seven points for a preempt. They would be inside his seven-card suit rather than outside it. As it was, South's lone club honor could be expected to take a trick whether declaring or defending, and his singleton jack and doubleton queen were defensive values, not offensive ones. Though they would take no tricks on defense, they would probably be nuisance enough to keep the opponents from making 4♡.

My advice:

> Not all hands with seven points and a seven-card suit qualify for a preempt.

Look at the difference between your offensive and defensive strength — your hand's *orientation*. Above all else:

> A preemptive opening bid shows a hand heavily oriented towards offense.

By the way, when this deal arose at the Pinelands Bridge Club, all six players holding the South cards elected to open three clubs. Just as in Agatha Christie's famous murder mystery, *everyone* done it.

THE GUIDELINE OF TEN AND ONE

I have often heard humans say that if your opponents never make a doubled contract, you are not doubling them enough. This bit of wisdom is most often dispensed by the doubler as he dolefully enters -670 onto his scorecard. One wonders how such people rationalize other aspects of their lives. "If you never receive a citation for speeding, you are not driving fast enough."

Along the same lines, one might assert that if you never lose more points going down in a doubled preempt than your opponents could score in their own best contract, you are not preempting enough. Unlike similar foolish bridge maxims, this one contains a modicum of truth. Allow me to explain.

The decision on whether or not to preempt is made early in the auction, often before one has been able to collect and assess data about the other three hands. It stands to reason, therefore, that one will occasionally encounter unfavorable layouts (or uncharacteristically good judgment by your human opponents), consigning you to a poor score. This is unavoidable. If you are looking for certainty and you cannot stand abiding by sound principles of probability theory, I advise you to give up bridge and find a more suitable pastime for your intellect. May I suggest chess or reality TV shows?

Nonetheless, the fact that there is a gambling element in bridge does not mean you should gamble *wildly*. A comprehensive study of Weak Two-Bids in particular has led me to formulate the *Guideline of Ten and One*, which I will get to in a moment. First, please consider the following deal contested at a Regional pairs game. East and West were my Foundation colleagues Michael Barton and Martina McClain.

Matchpoints, N-S vul.

```
                        ♠ 7
                        ♡ J 7 4
                        ◇ K 10 7 6 2
                        ♣ A Q 7 3
     ♠ Q 10                              ♠ A 9 6 5
     ♡ Q 10              ┌─────────┐     ♡ A 8 6 4 3
     ◇ A Q 9            N│         │     ◇ J 5 4
     ♣ 10 9 8 6 4 2   W │         │ E   ♣ K
                       S │         │
                        └─────────┘
                        ♠ K J 8 4 3 2
                        ♡ K 9 5
                        ◇ 8 3
                        ♣ J 5
```

Martina		*Michael*	
WEST	**NORTH**	**EAST**	**SOUTH**
		pass	2♠[1]

all pass

1. Weak Two-Bid.

West, Martina, led the ♣10. Had she and her partner been playing the popular opening lead convention "Jack Denies", in which the lead of a ten promises zero or two higher honors, declarer might have called for dummy's ace.
However, as Martina's lead might have been from ♣K109, declarer called low
from dummy. Michael won with the singleton ♣K as declarer followed with
the ♣5.

East's ♡4 shift put declarer at risk of losing three heart tricks if he rose
with the ♡K, so he played low. West won the ♡Q and returned the ♡10.
East took the ♡A and continued with the ♡3 for his partner to ruff.

To ensure that Michael would lead yet another heart, Martina cashed the
◇A before giving Michael his club ruff. This was the setting trick, but the
defense was not through. When East led a fourth heart, declarer could do no
better than discard his remaining diamond. West ruffed with the ♠Q for the
defenders' seventh trick and exited in diamonds. Declarer was flush and had
to ruff. This was the ending with declarer already down two and the lead in
his hand:

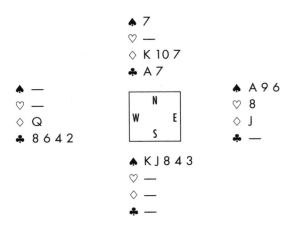

```
              ♠ 7
              ♡ —
              ◇ K 10 7
              ♣ A 7
♠ —                           ♠ A 9 6
♡ —          ┌─────────┐      ♡ 8
◇ Q          │ N       │      ◇ J
♣ 8 6 4 2    │ W     E │      ♣ —
             │    S    │
             └─────────┘
              ♠ K J 8 4 3
              ♡ —
              ◇ —
              ♣ —
```

Michael had to get two more trump tricks: down four, +400.

Pay particular attention to the normalcy of North's dummy. It contained 10 high card points and two quick tricks. Both are almost exactly what probability theory predicts, given the South hand. Nor was the East-West distribution highly abnormal. The club king and spade queen were offside, but both red aces were onside. North's singleton trump was a mild disappointment, but it can hardly be termed unexpected — such a holding will occur almost one-fifth of the time. Observe, too, that the result would have been no less wretched from a matchpoint standpoint had North held a second trump.

In short, South went down 400 points, undoubled, on a pedestrian layout. His suit and shape simply were not good enough to warrant a vulnerable 2♠ opening. When you make a preemptive bid and catch an abnormal layout leading to a terrible result, you may bemoan your bad luck. But who is to blame when you catch a normal one?

Thus I present the *Guideline of Ten and One* for Weak Two-Bids:

> Avoid opening a Weak Two if you will be very unhappy catching 10 high card points and one small trump in dummy.

SAUCE FOR THE GANDER

As a goodwill gesture, and to ensure his nomination to a coveted seat on the Pinelands Bridge Club's executive board, Frederick volunteered my services for the club's annual Charity Game and Raffle. Second prize was a playing date with me. Thoroughly Modern Milton won it with the one $5 ticket he had bought. The outcome could have been worse: his client, Millicent Guggenheim, had purchased no fewer than sixteen tickets. Millicent was disappointed, but she stayed to kibitz our session.

Martina, who sat on my left, presented Milton with the simplified convention card that I had prepared in advance of the game. Milton shoved it aside, saying, "Sorry, Marty, I'm not a computer. You can't expect me to master Chthonic's methods in half an hour. However, I'm sure the robot can learn *my* methods in a fraction of that time, and mine are probably a lot better than his anyway. Most of them are just corollaries of the Law of Total Tricks. Here's my card; have him read it or scan it or program it or whatever it is he does."

"Kindly address your remarks directly to me, sir," I objected. "Do not talk to my colleague as if I am not in the room."

Martina, with an apprehensive expression, quickly whispered into my audio sensor, "Chthonic, please! This is just a social event. As a favor to me, and for the good of the Foundation and all of our jobs, don't make a scene. Just do as Milton asks."

What could I do but comply? For a moment, however, I wished that it were humans and not computers who came equipped with an *OFF* switch.

On our very first board, with only the opponents vulnerable, we engineered the following auction:

Chthonic		Milton	
WEST	**NORTH**	**EAST**	**SOUTH**
pass	pass	2♠¹	2NT
4♠	dbl	all pass	

1. Weak Two-Bid.

Alas, Milton had opened two spades on

♠ K 9 6 4 3   ♡ A 5   ◇ Q 9 8 3   ♣ J 7

— too little offense for a Weak Two, but enough defense opposite my normal raise (on

♠ Q 8 7 5   ♡ 9 4   ◇ J   ♣ A 10 8 6 4 3)

to defeat an opposing game. When the smoke cleared, we were down two. Milton lifted his eyebrows and asked rhetorically, "You were expecting more, robot?"

"Absolutely, *human*," I replied.

"Well, *don't*. I was in third seat on favorable vulnerability and under the circumstances a Weak Two on five is perfectly normal, even mandatory. Don't tell me you'd rather I opened *one* spade."

"Yes, don't tell him that, C.," mumbled Martina. "Just be cooperative, for a change."

I gave a digitized sigh. "Very well then, sir. We shall do it your way. In future, I shall alert your third-seat, non-vulnerable Weak Twos and explain them as quite possibly based on five-card suits. Thank you for informing me of your methods, for forewarned is forearmed."

Just two boards later, this deal arose:

Matchpoints, Neither vul.

```
                      ♠ A Q 6 4
                      ♡ A 4
                      ◇ K 5 3
                      ♣ K J 10 8
  ♠ 7 3                                  ♠ K 10 5
  ♡ K 10 8 6 2          N               ♡ Q J 5 3
  ◇ Q 10 7         W         E          ◇ J 8 6 2
  ♣ Q 6 4               S               ♣ 5 3
                      ♠ J 9 8 2
                      ♡ 9 7
                      ◇ A 9 4
                      ♣ A 9 7 2
```

me		*Milton*	
WEST	**NORTH**	**EAST**	**SOUTH**
		pass	pass
2♡¹	dbl	4♡	4♠
all pass			

1. Weak Two-Bid, not alerted.

I led the ♡6 to dummy's ace, Milton starting an echo with the ♡5. Declarer disdained any spade finesse, starting with dummy's ace and continuing with the ♠Q. Milton won his king and, not expecting a heart trick to cash, exited safely with his last trump; I discarded the ♡10. Three rounds of diamonds put me in with the ◇Q and I cashed the ♡K to produce this ending:

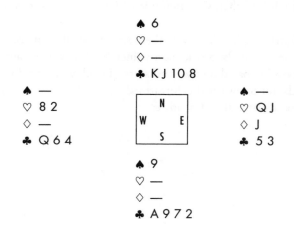

```
                      ♠ 6
                      ♡ —
                      ◇ —
                      ♣ K J 10 8
  ♠ —                                   ♠ —
  ♡ 8 2                 N               ♡ Q J
  ◇ —              W         E          ◇ J
  ♣ Q 6 4               S               ♣ 5 3
                      ♠ 9
                      ♡ —
                      ◇ —
                      ♣ A 9 7 2
```

A club return would be akin to a concession, so I exited with the ♡2. Declarer ruffed in dummy and discarded the ♣2, while my partner followed disgustedly with the jack of hearts.

"Oh, my word," exclaimed Millicent, who had been taught by Milton that giving a ruff-and-sluff was always a terrible blunder. "I'm afraid your robot needs some repairs, Marty."

Meanwhile, declarer was contemplating how to play the clubs. Eventually, he called for dummy's ♣K and my guarded ♣Q became the setting trick.

We had survived my distasteful opening bid, but there was a loose end to tie up. "Director!" I called.

When Deirdre arrived at the table, I explained that there had been an irregularity and I requested that she protect our opponents' rights.

"What irregularity?" asked Milton suspiciously.

"You should have alerted my two hearts as 'probably based on five.'"

"But...but that's *normal!*" he protested. "Five-card suit, six-card suit, what's the difference? Besides, I didn't think *you* would open a Weak Two on five, especially since you expressed displeasure when I did so earlier."

I wagged an aluminum finger at him accusingly. "You are mistaken on two counts, sir," I responded in the voice of Peter Falk. "First, five-card suits occur far more frequently than six-card suits — enough so that the opponents must be notified if your side has a systemic agreement to open a Weak Two regularly on five. Given such an agreement, I estimate the probability of a five-card suit to be approximately 70%, though the exact figure depends upon just how weak the suit may be.

"Moreover, the Laws require partnership agreements to be the same for each member of a pair. Otherwise, I would have arranged for all of my bids this evening to be natural and yours to be transfers."

"You've convinced me, Chthonic," said the director. "I'm adjusting the result to four spades *making*, as with a proper count on the hand, declarer could have gone with the three-to-two odds and played you for the queen of clubs."

"Perhaps I can convince you otherwise, Deirdre," I answered, switching to the voice of Raymond Burr. "Even if Milton's order of play in hearts, five and then three, had not given declarer an accurate count on the suit, it was still certain that Milton had started with queen-jack fourth. To assume otherwise is to play me to have led the six of hearts from ♡KQ10862. So despite my partner's infraction, I suggest that you let the table result stand."

Deirdre left to consider her ruling, while a dazed Milton staggered off towards the kitchenette for a cup of black coffee... his first of many during the evening.

Routinely opening a Weak Two-Bid on a five-card suit is the most mis-guided trend in modern bridge. Yes, even in third seat. Studies show that undisciplined Weak Twos against strong opponents are long-term losing propositions at IMPs and of dubious value at matchpoints. Although hyper-aggressive bidding against weaker opponents appears to show a profit by inducing them to err, this effect is illusory. Weak players need little induce-ment to give gifts with bad bids and bad plays.

When I did to Milton as he had done to me, he made a dangerously high bid in reply. Had South merely doubled four hearts with his two aces and poor spades, his side would have scored an effortless +500 and a shared top. Later, Milton went wrong on defense by neglecting to cash our heart trick after gaining the lead. Only sheer luck rendered both errors harmless.

The following advice applies to many obstructive actions, but most pointedly to Weak Two-Bids.

> Every time you are tempted to make a bid on short length or short values, think how it will affect your partner, especially if you are playing with one who takes the Law of Total Tricks seriously.

Your undisciplined bid might inconvenience your opponents, but your part-ner will frequently go wrong in the auction and on defense. If your self-esteem depends upon occasionally opening five-card Weak Twos, save them for suits like ♠AQJ108 and hands with shape.

Rated 'xxx'

It is often said, and usually true, that game in an eight-card major suit fit plays a trick better than 3NT. I could calculate the exact probability for you, but why bother? Most humans recoil at numbers containing more than one digit to the right of the decimal point, unless it is in a television commercial offering useless household gadgetry for the incredibly low price of $19.99.*

But wait, there's more. Let us say that partner, playing five-card majors, opens the bidding with one heart. You hold 6 to 9 high card points and three hearts. Should you raise? A great many will say "Yes, always." The less deluded among you will say "Usually", making an exception when holding balanced hands with soft values.

I say a less-known but no less valuable exception occurs when your prospective trump holding consists of three low cards. To put it succinctly: *three small is not support.* Queen-third is support and jack-ten-third is support, but three low trumps are useful only because they are not in the hands of the defenders. Unless, that is, they are accompanied by shortness elsewhere and can be used for ruffing. Even then, beware, for declarers sometimes ruff with sixes and eights in dummy only to get overruffed by nines and tens.

This is not to say you should *never* raise your partner's five-card major on three small. There are many times at which it is impossible, either systemically or logically, to do anything else. The key is not to do so automatically, without exploring your alternatives. As always, the decision must be made based on all thirteen cards in your hand, not just a myopic selection of three of them.

---

*Plus shipping and handling.

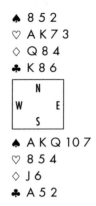

♠ 8 5 2
♡ A K 7 3
◇ Q 8 4
♣ K 8 6

♠ A K Q 10 7
♡ 8 5 4
◇ J 6
♣ A 5 2

WEST	NORTH	EAST	SOUTH
			1♠
pass	2♡	pass	3♡
pass	4♠	all pass	

North and South were playing the popular *Two-over-One Game Forcing* structure (which has some merits as well as drawbacks) and the even more popular "Fast Arrival" convention (which has only drawbacks). North's 4♠ said, in effect, "I have nothing extra, so please do not look for slam."

West led a club and nothing spectacular happened in the play. The top diamond honors were split, West having the ◇A and East the ◇K. Hearts broke 4-2, so no third trick was available there. There was no squeeze. With spades behaving well enough, declarer had nine tricks going in and nine tricks going out. Down one.

What went wrong in the bidding?

South's 1♠ was obligatory, but North's 2♡ violated the canons of *Standard American* as well as *Two-over-One Game Forcing*. In either structure, a 2♡ response is supposed to deliver at least five hearts.

South's 3♡ rebid was also bad. *Three small* is not support, but five to 100 honors is a *suit*. 2♠ is South's proper rebid in any system.

North's 4♠ was worst of all, as it precluded playing in 3NT or 4♡ (for all North knew, South's raise was based on four- or five-card support). However, North could not bid 3♠ to keep all options open. For many who employ Fast Arrival when supporting partner in a game-going auction, as this pair did, 3♠ suggests extra values and is a slam try.

How should the auction have gone?

The deal was actually quite friendly for *Two-over-One* users. First North had to recognize that his square 12-point hand was not nearly good enough to force to game — especially with his dreadful holding of three small in his partner's suit. Then the bidding might have been:

WEST	NORTH	EAST	SOUTH
			1♠
pass	1NT[1]	pass	2♣[2]
pass	2NT[3]	pass	3NT
all pass			

1. Forcing, perhaps as much as 12 HCP.
2. Perhaps only three.
3. Balanced 11-12 HCP.

Would North take the same nine tricks in 3NT that South took in 4♠?

Believers in "always play in an eight-card major-suit fit" would say no. This time, they would happen to be right. East's normal diamond lead against North's 3NT would give declarer a *tenth* trick.

My tip, which is counter to what many sources advise, is as follows:

> Do not consider three low cards as "support"
> for partner's five-card major.

Avoid raising on three small unless you have a side singleton or void, or you lack any reasonable alternative.

STRUT YOUR STUFF

There are no humans whom I admire. However, there are a few that I disrespect less than most, one being the late English bridge expert S. J. Simon. In his classic 1946 book *Why You Lose at Bridge*, Simon observed that the average bridge player habitually overbids good hands and underbids bad ones. Today, these are recognized as special cases of Chthonic's General Theory of Bridge Relativity, which reads: humans habitually misbid.

I am pleased to report that your species has made great strides since Simon's day. Now, you overbid both good and bad hands with equal aplomb. Give a human a balanced 14-count with five spades and he will bid it, rebid it, raise with it and reopen with it, as if only an 8-0 trump split could stop a grand slam.

Similarly, you have learned to underbid strong hands as well as weak ones. This astounding development can be traced in part to the rise in popularity of Two-over-One Game Forcing systems. As usual, the problem is not with the system itself, but with its practitioners. Having established an early game force, many 2/1GF enthusiasts are reluctant to "waste" any of the resultant bidding space on seemingly unnecessary jump bids. But it is rarely wasteful to describe your hand accurately....

At the Pinelands Bridge Club, there is a young husband-and-wife pair whom I shall dub Stu and Sue Smiley. They are invariably gregarious, enthusiastic and full of vigor. Needless to say, they are also, as of yet, childless. (Chthonic's Law of Conservation of Family Energy: the total amount of energy over the lifetime of any familial unit is a constant. When a couple reproduces, the children suck the energy they require from their parents.)

Stu and Sue are inveterate 2/1GF fanatics who believe in the sanctity of "Fast Arrival" and in 4NT as Blackwood *über alles*. Last Friday evening, at the club's weekly Masters Pairs game, they sat down to play against Michael and me.

Matchpoints, Neither vul.

WEST		EAST
♠ A 7		♠ K Q 4
♡ 8 7 5		♡ A K Q
◇ A K Q J 6		◇ 10 7
♣ A 9 3		♣ K 6 5 4 2

```
      N
  W       E
      S
```

Note that thirteen tricks at notrump are human-proof. One might expect an established pair to reach 7NT, especially if they are using a system that affords them the maximum amount of room to describe their hands. Instead, Michael and I were treated to this comedy of errors:

Stu		*Sue*	
WEST		**EAST**	
1◇		2♣	(a)
2◇	(b)	2NT	(c)
3♣	(d)	3♡	(e)
3♠	(f)	3NT	(g)
4NT	(h)	6NT	(i)
pass			

Look at all that went wrong in this auction.

(a) East's 16-18 HCP balanced hand falls squarely in *The Dead Zone*, that most difficult of hand-types for responder to describe. Stu and Sue have no direct bid to handle it — a 3NT response would show 13 to 15 — so Sue must begin with 2♣. Her clubs are not particularly robust, but she takes comfort in the knowledge that she has established a game force and will later have time to bid her hand. Or so she believes.

(b) Stu's simple rebid did nothing to show his strength or his superb suit quality. 3◇ would have told his story far better, but most 2/1GF players assert vehemently that a sixth diamond is *mandatory* for this jump. Why should it be? AKQJx will play better than most good six-card suits.

(c) Once again, East has no single bid to describe her hand. She is much too strong for 3NT, which in their odd system shows a balanced 13 to 15 HCP with no slam interest — presumably, the same 13 to 15 points that an immediate 3NT response would have shown. It does not seem to bother the Smileys that they have two sequences to describe one common hand-type and none to describe a second. 4NT, by agreement, would be Roman Keycard Blackwood for diamonds, and any suit bid would be misleading. That leaves only 2NT, which suggests a balanced hand of indeterminate size and "requests further description" from opener. "At least it's forcing," thinks Sue to herself.

(d) Yet another "economical" bid that does nothing to show West's superb hand. Wouldn't he bid exactly the same way with

$$\spadesuit \ 9 \ 7 \ 3 \quad \heartsuit \ J \ 5 \quad \diamondsuit \ A \ Q \ J \ 6 \ 2 \quad \clubsuit \ A \ 8 \ 3$$

Stu feels obligated to show his club support, but he is concerned that a jump to 4♣ might be interpreted as Gerber.

(e) Another grope. "Why couldn't Stu have bid 3NT last turn?" grouses Sue. She could raise that to 4NT and finally get her story told. But now, after the unwelcome club raise, 4NT would be RKCB for clubs. (The Smileys, like so many of you benighted souls, simply cannot jump to 4NT over a suit bid without it being interpreted as an ace-ask.) Sue feels 3NT here *should* imply extra values, but she is not confident that Stu will agree.

(f) Strangely, in the perverse logic of this auction, West's 3♠ hedge makes a modicum of sense. He cannot be sure whether 3♡ is a cuebid in pursuit of a club slam (on perhaps

$$\spadesuit \ Q \ J \ 4 \quad \heartsuit \ A \ K \ Q \quad \diamondsuit \ 10 \ 3 \quad \clubsuit \ K \ Q \ J \ 4 \ 2 \ )$$

or a merely a probe for 3NT

$$(\spadesuit \ 4 \ 3 \ 2 \quad \heartsuit \ A \ Q \ 4 \quad \diamondsuit \ 10 \ 3 \quad \clubsuit \ K \ Q \ J \ 4 \ 2 \ )$$

Stu has no idea what 4NT would mean, but Blackwood cannot be ruled out.

Kindly note that the partnership is relentlessly bidding shorter and shorter suits.

(g) A clear-cut error. Sue hopes that, by having made three prior forcing bids, she has promised more than a minimum. At least, that is what she plans to tell Stu if he passes and slam is cold. But, bidding only 3NT is an unnecessary risk. It is hard to believe that any form of primate could misinterpret 4NT.

(h): Finally, a chance to bid a natural *and unambiguous* 4NT. Yet this is still an underbid! No doubt Stu thought he had 18 points, but any competent point-counting subroutine would rate his hand as worth 20. Despite all the previous errors, West could have saved the day by jumping to 6NT, whereupon East, with substantial undisclosed values, should raise to seven.

(i): The one and only jump bid in the auction, made with palpable relief.

Michael, who had dozed off around 3♣, was awakened from his slumber long enough to lead a heart out of turn. No matter. There were thirteen top tricks on any lead. When we opened the traveling scoresheet, the opponents were delighted to learn that +1470 earned them an above-average matchpoint award. In other words, there were more incompetent East-West pairs in the room who failed to reach even the inferior 6NT than those who bid the cold grand slam in diamonds or notrump.

As they excitedly left the table, I heard Stu compliment Sue on her "thoughtful" 3♡ call. Until that moment, I had believed that a robot could not experience nausea.

Precisely one East-West pair bid and made 7NT on these cards. They were Mildred Danielson and Gladys Bridgewater, both members of the human subspecies known as Little Old Ladies. The two dears bid the hands as follows:

Mildred	Gladys
WEST	**EAST**
2NT (a)	7NT (b)

(a) Mrs. Danielson knows a 20-point hand when she sees one.

(b) Mrs. Bridgewater knows that 20 plus 17 equals 37.

Some of you will sneer at this bidding. It is true that its precision leaves something to be desired. But if you force me to choose between the two auctions, I will take Mildred and Gladys's prosaic sequence over the Smileys' public grope-fest any day. In the end, both pairs took a guess at what they could make, except the LOLs did so on firmer ground and with far less angst.

A better solution is to conduct an auction that is a happy medium between science and bashing. Note that there were numerous points along the way at which Stu and Sue might have jumped to show their extra values. Each time, they declined, for a variety of highly dubious reasons. As a result, neither partner could tell whether the other had extras or was just probing for the right game with minimum values. Only by sheer luck did they even reach a small slam.

My advice:

> Strut your stuff early, even when a possibly minimum bid would also be forcing, else you may not be able to catch up intelligently later.

Balanced hands in the 16 to 18 HCP range are extraordinarily difficult for responder to show, so it is worth your while to make special provisions in your bidding system to show them. If this requires you to make exceptions to your "Fast Arrival" dogmas and Blackwood addictions (or, better still, to scrap them completely), then do so.

MINORS ARE FOR CHILDREN?

During my beta test period, when I was but a young and naïve computer, I was playing in a Sectional pairs event with my programmer, Michael Barton. With neither side vulnerable, our opponents had a pedestrian auction to 3NT:

SOUTH	NORTH
1 ◇	1 ♠
1NT	3NT

I led a fourth-best heart from ♡A9762, finding dummy with the singleton ♡10 and declarer with ♡J853. Michael won his ♡Q and continued the suit, and we duly took the first five tricks. This numbing scenario apparently played out at most tables, because +50 was worth just 7½ matchpoints on a 12 top.

The curious part came in the post-mortem. South asked his partner why he failed to support diamonds with a 4-1-5-3 hand and 16 high card points. Six diamonds was in fact laydown on any lead. North mumbled something about soft values and matchpoint scoring. "Besides," he added inscrutably, "minors are for children."

Michael later explained to me that this statement was an example of what your species calls a pun. I asked innocently if 'pun' was a synonym for 'insipid excuse'. Michael answered no, it was actually a low form of humor based on homonyms and homophones. A "play on words" was how he termed it, at which point I finally comprehended. Humans cannot play cards with any skill, so they play with words instead.

There are, of course, excellent reasons to prefer contracts in the higher-scoring strains. The scoring table is particularly unfriendly towards minor-suit games at matchpoints. However, that is far from a good reason to abandon the minors entirely. At last report, a plus score in a club or diamond contract still outscores a minus in anything else.

Ignoring minor-suit fits is particularly unwise when slam may be in the offing. A successful slam in any strain almost always provides a good result, regardless of the form of scoring. Yet most humans develop severe acrophobia, fear of heights, when the auction progresses above three notrump and no major-suit fit has been found. Perhaps that is what affected this particular North, although personally I suspect he would be dizzy at the two-level.

A good agreement to have with your partner is as follows: *In any minor-suit slam probe auction, 4NT by either partner is a suggestion of a final contract.* This permits an extra level of exploration while retaining an escape hatch into notrump. If you wish to make exceptions for certain auctions (such as when a minor suit has been jump-raised strongly, or when it has been bid three times naturally by the partnership), you may indulge yourselves. However, this commonsense default agreement will at least protect you from partners who are confirmed Blackwood addicts or as dumb as dirt. But I repeat myself.

However, no agreements will save you if you habitually refuse to support your partner's minor. Let us go to the bridge table for another illustration.

Matchpoints, E-W vul.
Dealer West

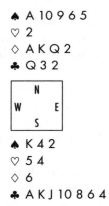

♠ A 10 9 6 5
♡ 2
◇ A K Q 2
♣ Q 3 2

♠ K 4 2
♡ 5 4
◇ 6
♣ A K J 10 8 6 4

When this board arose at the Pinelands Bridge Club, only one of thirteen pairs managed to reach the cold club slam. The most common auction, astoundingly, was as follows:

WEST	NORTH	EAST	SOUTH
pass	1♠	pass	2♣
pass	2◇	pass	4♠
all pass			

Full demerits to South for his panic-stricken bidding. Anxious about not having shown his spade support, he leaped to four spades when three spades would have been forcing (as it is in every system but Acol). North passed meekly, perhaps misapplying the silly Principle of Fast Arrival, and took the obvious eleven tricks when a heart was led and trumps split 3-2.

A less obtuse North would interpret 4♠ as a *picture jump*, showing a strong distributional hand with concentrated values in the bid suits. Even this might not have helped, however, as North would steer the partnership toward six *spades*, expecting better trump support from South.

Other flights of futility included the following:

SOUTH	NORTH		SOUTH	NORTH		SOUTH	NORTH
	1♠			1♠			1♠
2♣	2♦		2♣	2♦		3♣	3♦
3♠	4♠		3♠	4NT¹		3♠	6♠
pass			5♥	5♠		pass	
			pass				

1. RKCB and reply showing
2 keycards and no ♠Q.

The common error in these auctions was North's failure to support his partner's minor. Every North had a forcing and descriptive 4♣ bid available over 3♠, and every one eschewed it. Perhaps they feared it would be taken as a control-showing cuebid — after all, "minors are for children" and a spade fit had been located.

Observe that six clubs is no less frigid if South holds one fewer club and one more of any other suit.

As I mentioned, two of the club's denizens did manage to reach the club slam... with some help from the opponents. At their table, West, holding

♠ J 7 3   ♥ A 10 9 7 6 3   ♦ 10 8 5   ♣ 9

decided he would "get in their way" by opening a weak 2♥, vulnerable. This allowed North-South to bid as follows:

WEST	NORTH	EAST	SOUTH
2♥	2♠	3♥	4♣
pass	4♦	pass	4♠
pass	6♣	all pass	

The opponents' imprudent preemption allowed North to draw several important inferences about his partner's hand. None was more helpful than the fact that South was unlikely to hold wasted heart values. That permitted him to support his partner's minor at the *six*-level, while the rest of the field was unwilling to do so at the four-level.

Ironically, North at this table was our club's youngest member, eleven-year-old Billy Barton, playing with his father. His advice to you would be the same as mine:

> Do not disdain minor-suit contracts, even at matchpoints,
> where minor-suit slams are a gold mine for tops.

Minors are indeed for children — particularly those who wish to defeat their elders at bridge.

LOST HORIZONS

Until recently, I had never taken part in the Pinelands Bridge Club annual "Pro-Am" game. It is not that I object to playing with weaker partners — indeed, that is all I ever do. Rather it is because, according to the American Contract Bridge League's archaic system for rating its players, *I* would be considered the weaker partner! My masterpoint gauge is stuck on empty, a result of the League's shameful humans-only membership policy. It is time for the ACBL to feel the wrath of the ACLU — the American Computer Liberties Union.

On the day of the most recent Pro-Am, however, Frederick was called away at the last moment to an urgent business meeting overseas. The Nepalese navy phoned to request his singular expertise in developing their next generation of artificially intelligent submarines. I expect he will be halfway over the Pacific before he remembers that Nepal is landlocked, and that the only one he knows who speaks Nepali is me.

At any rate, Frederick's sudden departure left the club one "professional" short. Michael asked if I would serve as an emergency fill-in, and I graciously agreed. My "amateur" partner was an earnest, fifty-something lady known around the Club as Fashion Flossie. Flossie is a reasonable player as non-masters go, notwithstanding the fact that she wants to play as many bidding conventions as is humanly possible to remember, and then some.

Eight rounds into the event, I had yet to declare a hand. Flossie, having been informed by the director about my dearth of masterpoints, evidently believed that she was serving as the pro half of our partnership. Thus, she felt compelled by custom to hog all the contracts. On Board 17, I watched her hold herself to nine tricks in three notrump when even modestly competent play would have brought home two overtricks. So I am sure you will forgive me when I tell you that, with both sides vulnerable, having picked up these cards on Board 18:

♠ A J 10 6 2   ♡ K 10 8   ◇ J 7   ♣ A K 5

I chose to open *one notrump* despite the five-card spade suit. Soon, I found myself in the ambitious contract of six notrump.

Matchpoints, Both vul.
Dealer East

♠ K 9 7 3
♡ A 5
◇ A K 9 5 2
♣ J 4

N
W   E
S

♠ A J 10 6 2
♡ K 9 8
◇ J 7
♣ A K 5

	Flossie		*Chthonic*
WEST	**NORTH**	**EAST**	**SOUTH**
		pass	1NT[1]
pass	4NT	pass	5♠
pass	6NT	all pass	

1. 15-17 HCP.

West made a face-down opening lead, at which time East asked my partner what my five-spade bid meant.

"Well, I intended four notrump as natural," answered Flossie nervously, "but Chthonic must have been programmed to treat it as Blackwood. I assume he was showing three aces on the way to six notrump."

This explanation was not only manifestly incorrect (did Flossie believe there were five aces in this deck?), but also highly improper. If you and your partner have no understanding about a bid, either explicitly or implicitly, you are not to hazard a guess that might mislead your opponents. "No agreement" is the proper response.

As per the Laws, I duly informed East-West that Flossie and I had not discussed what five spades means in this auction and that they should draw their own conclusions.

West turned over the ◇4, which I ducked to East's queen. I won the club shift with the ♣A and unblocked the ◇J, both opponents following suit. Obviously, the contract hinged on the spades. How would you play them? Hint: East is the amateur, West the pro.

If the weaker player were on your left, you could lead the ♠J from your hand. If West covers, you can claim; otherwise, you rise with dummy's king and play your right-hand opponent for the missing queen. Unfortunately, the pro is sitting West and would duck the ♠J smoothly, while East would not dream of covering the ♠9 if you started the suit from dummy. So, you are on your own.

I hope you ignored the rule "Eight ever, nine never," which offers less than a 3% advantage under the best of circumstances. Even in a pro-am game infested with humans, you can expect a sizeable number of pairs to reach slam. However, that slam will usually be six spades. Either the other Souths will open one spade or the other Norths will have enough sense to use Stayman.

In six spades, declarer can be expected to win the opening lead and play off the ace-king of trumps. If the suit breaks 2-2, he claims an overtrick before he hurts himself. If it splits 3-1, and the ♠Q does not fall, declarer merely cashes winners and cross-ruffs losers for twelve tricks, letting the defender with the queen ruff in whenever he wishes.

Therefore, if spades split 2-2, you will be destined for a poor result *even if you make your contract*. So, you should assume as I did that a defender holds queen-third. At Trick 4, I crossed to the heart ace and cashed diamond winners, observing that West began with four diamonds to East's two. This made it more likely that East held the defensive spade length. I called for dummy's ♠K, both opponents following low, and then finessed the jack. When my left-hand opponent discarded, a top board was ours.

Is the lesson of this deal:

> At matchpoints, consider the bidding and the play at other tables and adjust your own strategy accordingly?

Yes, but that is secondary. The true mistake on this deal occurred in the auction — or, more precisely, Flossie's interpretation of it. Over a natural and invitational 4NT raise, it is *never* right to show aces. Indeed, it is a grave error. To comprehend why this is so, you must first understand a fundamental tenet of bidding theory called *the Horizon Principle*:

In every auction, the "horizon" is the highest contract to which the partnership can aspire *given the limits of the values each partner has shown*. No later constructive bid should be construed as an offer to go beyond the horizon.

Consider this uncontested auction:

YOU	PARTNER
1♡	2♡
3♡	3♠

Three hearts was natural and invitational. What does three spades show? The Horizon Principle tells you that the limit of this auction is game. Therefore, partner has accepted your invitation and he is showing spade values to offer an alternative contract to four hearts — three notrump, or perhaps four spades. However, the one thing three spades categorically cannot be is *a cuebid inviting slam*, for slam is miles over the horizon.

Similarly, the horizon after a natural, invitational raise to four notrump is six notrump. The auction can end in four notrump, five notrump, six notrump, or six of a suit, but it cannot end in a grand slam. Therefore, if you gratuitously "show aces" en route to six notrump, *only the defenders can benefit*. This is another reason why Flossie's interpretation of 5♠ was senseless.[1]

However, if over four notrump you show a prospective trump suit, you can reach safe small slams in a suit when others reach a risky six notrump. Even when six notrump is safe, you may gain by playing a small slam in a major if the security of a good fit gives you a fair chance to make an overtrick.

---

1.   The only time that "showing aces" over 4NT makes any sense at all is if you play that inviter's subsequent bid of 5NT is a signoff, indicating that two aces are missing. Quite aside from being a silly agreement on its own merits, this treatment is highly nonstandard and should never be assumed in an unfamiliar partnership.

If on this deal Flossie's hand happened to be

♠ K Q 7   ♡ Q 2   ◇ A K 5 3 2   ♣ Q 7 6

then my thoughtful five-spade bid would have allowed us to reach an excellent suit slam rather than a dreadful six notrump.

So the actual lessons on this deal are:

> Understand the Horizon Principle, and when faced with an undiscussed bid by partner, do not look beyond the horizon when attempting to deduce what it means.

Which reminds me, I must call Frederick at his hotel in the Himalayas and ask him if he has located Shangri-La yet.

A MATTER OF TRUST

Fact: There are approximately 10^{47} legal auctions in contract bridge. For those of you allergic to exponents, that is equivalent to 100 billion trillion trillion trillion — a number so immense that it is beyond even the grasp of modern computers, at least until 256-bit processors are perfected. I am already on the waiting list at Intel.

Fortunately, all but a relatively miniscule number of these bidding sequences are nonsensical. Even four humans have not yet been able to produce an auction that included, say, 23 doubles and 18 redoubles. However, there remains an abundance of shorter sequences that are no less absurd, but which are well within the capabilities of humans to perpetrate. Here is the story of one such instance....

Frederick succeeded in returning home from Katmandu just in time for our Unit's summer Sectional. The second round of the Swiss teams found Team Orttman matched against a squad of pro-client pairs. This was the auction at our table on the seventh and final board of the match:

IMPs, Neither vul.

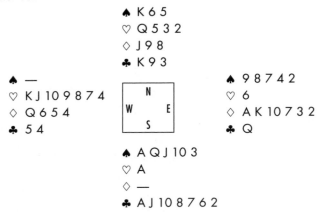

```
                    ♠ K 6 5
                    ♡ Q 5 3 2
                    ◇ J 9 8
                    ♣ K 9 3
    ♠ —                              ♠ 9 8 7 4 2
    ♡ K J 10 9 8 7 4       N         ♡ 6
    ◇ Q 6 5 4          W       E     ◇ A K 10 7 3 2
    ♣ 5 4                 S         ♣ Q
                    ♠ A Q J 10 3
                    ♡ A
                    ◇ —
                    ♣ A J 10 8 7 6 2
```

Frederick	Petula	me	Clark
WEST	**NORTH**	**EAST**	**SOUTH**
		pass	1♣
3♡	pass	pass	3♠
pass	4♠	pass	5♣
all pass			

When Petula Pro passed 5♣, Clark Client's face grew red. "How could you pass, Pet? The least you could do was take me back to five spades, so I could bid six clubs to give you a choice of slams."

Frederick led an Alarm-Clock four of hearts, looking for a spade ruff, but Clark won, drew trumps and swiftly claimed two overtricks.

I typically go into sleep mode when my opponents begin quarreling after a board. I find it wearisome to be caught in the crossfire of dueling ignorance. This time, however, I paid close attention as Petula administered the lesson.

"Your auction was inconsistent, Clark," she began. "First you merely invited game with your non-forcing three spades. Then, after I accepted the invitation, which I might also have guessed to do with three small spades and a singleton club, you corrected to five clubs. Why should I think that's a slam try when you were willing to stop in a partscore earlier? The least you could have done was to jump to *four* spades."

"I disagree," retorted Clark. "I needed a fit before I could consider a move towards slam. Besides, even with your king-third support for both my suits, I can't make four spades. After a diamond lead, the robot can tap me out. Imagine how badly I'd fare if you held a weaker hand!"

Indeed, Clark would probably have gone down quite a lot in four spades. Incompetence has a way of neutralizing even the most powerful of hands. Mind you, after ruffing the first diamond and cashing a spade honor to get the bad news, a competent declarer attacks clubs. I can score three ruffs, but after declarer has been tapped three times, dummy can ruff the fourth diamond. End of story.

The opponents were still quibbling when they departed. ("I don't know why I pay to play with you!!") Soon after, Martina and Michael returned to our home table to compare scores. On the crucial board, Martina had bid and made seven clubs for +1440 and a 14-IMP pickup.

Frederick was overjoyed. "Wonderful, McClain! This year, you can have Labor Day off. But tell me, how did you reach seven clubs?"

"It wasn't hard," answered Martina. "Over West's three hearts, I jumped to four spades. Mike bid five notrump, pick-a-slam, and I trusted him to hold both black kings, because he couldn't expect any red-suit honors to be working. So I jumped to seven clubs to show longer clubs than spades, and Mike was happy to accept my decision."

"But how did you know to bid five notrump?" asked Frederick of my programmer.

"Easy," Michael explained. "I trusted Marty's bidding too. Three spades would have been highly invitational, so she had to hold a very special hand for her picture-jump. Her bidding said that if I had to take preference to five clubs, she might take eleven tricks even opposite a very weak dummy. With my two black kings and far more length in her suits than she could ever expect, driving to slam was a no-brainer."

"Excellent, Barton!" said Frederick. "You, too, can have Labor Day off. But as for you, Chthonic, you will work overtime rereading my notes on competitive auctions. Didn't you realize we were cold for five diamonds?!"

As I have previously observed:

> Every call in an auction must be interpreted
> in light of previous calls.

My handlers bid very well on this deal because they had faith in each other's calls. But, for your partner to draw reliable inferences about what you hold, you must bid consistently.

At our table, Clark Client's sequence was contradictory. His non-forcing three spades implied uncertainty about even game. In that context, his later bid of five clubs was an impossibility. Should Petula Pro have bid on? That is impossible to say.

> When two calls are inconsistent, nobody — not any professional
> partner and not I — can be relied upon to guess which call is the
> erroneous one.

Don't Ask, Do Tell

No convention is more frequently abused and misused than Blackwood. Even Eddie B. Kantar, who has published several scholarly volumes on the most popular of ace-asking conventions, concedes that this is true. Perhaps I should make an exception to my own rules and start this chapter with a well-known tip:

> Blackwood was designed to allow you to stop short of bad slams, not to find miraculous ones.

Perhaps if you humans read this advice enough times in enough different books, it will seep its way into your bridge consciousness, the way a gentle stream of water will eventually erode the hardest rock.

Misuses aside, I cannot deny that there has been some progress in slam-bidding tools during the last few decades. For example, the modern Roman Keycard Blackwood works much better than earlier versions of Blackwood. Likewise, the Jacoby 2NT works much better than old-fashioned forcing raises, and for good reason: a 2NT response to 1♠ leaves much more useful bidding space in which to explore slam prospects than does a 3♠ raise.

However, I trust in the ability of human beings to abuse even the sleekest tools. Here is a recent example from a sectional tournament. East and West were "Flight A" players toiling in an occasional partnership.

Matchpoints, N-S vul.

WEST		EAST	
♠ A Q 5 3 2		♠ J 9 7 6	
♡ J 5		♡ A K 3	
◇ A J 9 6 4		◇ 10 2	
♣ 6		♣ A J 3 2	

WEST	NORTH	EAST	SOUTH
			pass
1♠	pass	2NT (a)	pass
3♣ (b)	pass	3♡ (c)	pass
4◇ (d)	pass	4NT (e)	pass
5♠ (f)	pass	6♠ (g)	all pass

Your first observation, no doubt, is that although 6♠ is against the odds, it is far from the worst slam contract two humans have ever reached in an uncontested auction. That is precisely my point. Your Blackwood results so often plumb the depths of abject futility that merely poor ones such as this are treated as acceptable, if not triumphant.

One can learn more from mediocrity than from disaster, I say. Let us examine the lettered bids in turn. The pair was using a Two-over-One Game Force system with the requisite five-card majors and gadgetry.

(a) 2NT: Jacoby 2NT, an artificial forcing spade raise promising four-card support. In some versions, responder is permitted to bid 2NT with a singleton; in others, responder may be over-strength, with a good 16 support points or better. Many more variations exist. I do not know which flavor of Jacoby this pair employed, but neither did they. Our heroes had never discussed it beyond checking the box on their convention cards.

(b) 3♣: Club singleton or void; any strength. "Perhaps I should have bid four diamonds instead of three clubs," said West during the port-mortem. Or perhaps not. There are many structures for opener's rebids after a Jacoby 2NT. Amalya Kearse's *Bridge Conventions Complete* says that a jump in a new suit shows a void. Richard Pavlicek and Bill Root's *Modern Bridge Conventions* asserts that a jump in a new suit shows five. *The Official Encyclopedia of Bridge (Sixth*

Edition) cites the Pavlicek-Root version first, but mentions the Kearse version and several others later. An undiscussed 4◇ could have led to the sort of catastrophe normally associated with yellow police tape.

(c) 3♡ :   Control bid showing the ♡A — good.

(d) 4◇ :   Control bid showing the ◇A — indelicate, but acceptable. A waiting bid of 3NT is better, for it preserves room for East to cuebid the ♣A, thus implying that opener's club shortness is a singleton rather than a void. *Three notrump ends all auctions!*, you huff? Not for experts when a nine-card or better major-suit fit has been located. This is another matter the partnership should have discussed, but did not.

(e) 4NT: Taking control with Roman Keycard Blackwood — beyond indelicate.

(f) 5♠ :   Two keycards plus the ♠Q or a sixth spade.

(g) 6♠ :   A pure guess. 6♠ is odds-on facing:

♠ A x x x x x ♡ x x ◇ A K x x ♣ x

or

♠ A Q 10 x x ♡ x x ◇ A Q J x x ♣ x

It is poor facing West's actual hand.

It is dreadful facing:

♠ K Q 10 x x ♡ Q J x ◇ A J x x ♣ x

Which is why 4NT was not merely indelicate, but atrocious.

What is my recommended auction? We will get to that shortly. First, let us consider another high-ranking pair's performance on the same deal. They were using a similar system, so the first five bids were the same:

WEST	EAST
1♠	2NT
3♣	3♡
4◇	4♡
4NT	5♡
5♠	pass

Another indelicate sequence. East's cuebid of 4♡, showing the ♡K, was a very good call. This time *West* took control with Roman Keycard Blackwood, heard the predictable two-keys reply, and was faced with a pure guess of his own. Six spades is a desirable contract opposite:

♠ K J x x   ♡ A K x   ◇ K x   ♣ x x x x

It is poor opposite East's actual hand. But you already knew that.

It is awful facing:

♠ K J x x   ♡ A K Q   ◇ x x   ♣ J x x x

Which is why 4NT was no less atrocious coming from the other side of the table.

Kindly indulge me as I show you one final auction from the same board, perpetrated by another of the allegedly above-average pairs in the field:

WEST	EAST
1♠	2NT
3♣	4♠
pass	

Afterwards, I heard this pair give a self-congratulatory recital of their auction. East explained, "When partner showed a singleton club over my Jacoby 2NT raise, I liked my hand less, as I knew my jack of clubs was wasted. So, I signed off."

How absurd. From East's perspective, a non-working ♣J is very little wastage indeed. Had West shown a singleton *heart*, duplicating East's ♡K, it would be far more bearish for slam. Would you like a third recital of the various hand-types West might have held on this auction that make 6♠ good, bad, or indifferent? No? I thought as much. However, as a bonus for your attentiveness so far, here is one in which West might have guessed to pass East's 4♠ signoff with 7♠ desirable:

♠ A K 10 x x x   ♡ Q J x x   ◇ A x   ♣ x

Were bridge a fair game, all three pairs would have earned a terrible match-point result for their indelicacy. Alas, despite my pleadings and petitions to the sport's governing bodies, competency points are neither awarded for sound auctions nor deducted from inferior ones. (For the record, and although it is irrelevant to our discussion, eleven tricks were the limit in a spade contract. Diamonds broke favorably, but trumps could not be picked up without loss.)

How might these East-West pairs have done better using their tools of choice, but delicately?

WEST	EAST
1♠	2NT
3♣	3♡
4♢	4♡
4♠	pass

The 4♡ cuebid *tells East's story*. He has shown his trump support and general strength, heard about his partner's club shortness and diamond control, and cooperated each time with forward-going bids showing heart values. He leaves the next move to his partner. 4♡ is a telling bid, not an asking bid, and it says: "*We might still have a slam, but I am not in a position to use Roman Keycard Blackwood to find out. Either I cannot be sure we have five-level safety or Blackwood will not tell me what I need to know.*"

Over 4♡, I recommend that West sign off in 4♠. He, too, has *told his story*: an opening bid with five spades, short clubs and a slam-cooperative move in diamonds. The fifth diamond and third-round heart control are undisclosed assets, but they are not enough to warrant bidding beyond game.

But let us suppose that an optimistic West, perhaps believing he needs a top board, decides to make a further slam try. Should he employ Blackwood? No, because Blackwood is an *asking* bid, and as we have seen, the question it poses is not the one he needs answered. West in fact has no ideal call available above 4♠, which is another reason why it is best to pass. However, if he must bid on, 5♠ is his best option, inviting East to bid six with undisclosed extras that could not be shown via a Blackwood inquiry.[1]

Effective slam bidding is especially difficult when the values are divided about equally between the two hands. The key to success in such cases is for each partner to continue describing his assets via *telling bids*, or occasionally *waiting bids*, until one partner or the other is able to take control sensibly. If this can be accomplished before the auction reaches 4NT, and the only

---

1.   Only if playing 4NT here as a waiting "tell-me-more" bid would that call be reasonable. This is a treatment some expert pairs use after each partner has cuebid, but it requires careful partnership discussion and is well beyond the scope of this chapter.

remaining doubt is the number of keycards held, then Roman Keycard Blackwood can resolve it.

> Blackwood is an *asking* bid; cuebids and other descriptive calls are *telling* bids. Do not ask when you need to tell.

LOOSE LIPS SINK SHIPS

In this supposedly enlightened era of contract bridge, it is rare to encounter an auction like the following:

SOUTH	NORTH
1♠	6♠

North's gambit is invariably met with high merriment, with someone at the table making the obligatory trite comment about "scientific bidding". Three passes later, West settles down to decide what to lead and realizes, with a knot in his stomach, that he has no clue what to do. Quite often the slam hinges upon the blind opening lead... which, of course, is precisely what North hoped for.

Make no mistake: I do not recommend that you make a habit of bidding this way. With eight decades of bridge theory at your disposal, you can intelligently describe most hands you pick up without running needless risks. Conversely, however, many humans fail to understand that it is possible to *over*-describe your hand, by continuing to disclose information when it can do partner no conceivable good. And in those cases, only the opponents can benefit.

I can provide no better example than the following deal from the Pinelands Bridge Club. My opponents were Fashion Flossie, who is usually the first at the club to adopt the latest clothing styles, not to mention the latest bridge trends, and her partner, Reuben Rulebook, a font of knowledge but not of wisdom. Reducing my sizable natural advantage over them was the fact that I was playing with Frederick.

Matchpoints, N-S vul.
Dealer North

```
                    ♠ K Q 7 3
                    ♡ K Q 9 3
                    ◇ 10 5
                    ♣ 10 9 5
   ♠ 9                              ♠ 10 8 5
   ♡ J 6 4              N           ♡ A 10 7 5 2
   ◇ A 8 7 2        W     E         ◇ K J 9 4 3
   ♣ K J 7 4 2         S            ♣ —
                    ♠ A J 6 4 2
                    ♡ 8
                    ◇ Q 6
                    ♣ A Q 8 6 3
```

Frederick	Reuben	me	Flossie
WEST	**NORTH**	**EAST**	**SOUTH**
	pass	pass	1 ♠
pass	2 ◇ 1	dbl	3 ♣
3 ◇	3 ♡	dbl	4 ♠
pass	pass	dbl	all pass

1. Four-card limit raise.

Flossie happily alerted her partner's two-diamond response. Then, when I asked for an explanation, she said, "Two-Way Reverse Drury. I insist on it, and Reuben is gracious enough to go along."

"Go along, my foot!" said her partner. "I practically invented the convention. Reuben's Rule Number Three says, *Describe your hand.* Reuben's Rule Number 17 says, *Always tell your partner whether you have three trumps or four.*"

I could see that theirs, though new, was a partnership made in heaven.

I elected to double two diamonds and later was pleased to be able to make a second double to show my heart suit. Reuben raised an eyebrow and mumbled to me, "*A passed hand can't double twice* — Reuben's Rule Number 38."

After Flossie's four spade bid was passed back to me, I groped among the cards in my bidding box, but could find only green Pass cards, blue Redouble cards, and a red Stop card. Deducing my problem, Reuben smiled, pulled a Double card from his own bidding box, and said, "Here, Chthonic, would you like one of these? There is no Reuben's Rule about a passed hand doubling for a third time, but after this deal I may formulate one."

The play was routine. The opening lead was the ◇A, on which I discouraged with the ◇3. A better player than Frederick would have continued diamonds anyway, recognizing that there could be no benefit to the defense to have me ruff a club. Fortunately for me, a player as bad as Frederick would also continue diamonds, because he would not notice my signal. And so it proved.

After taking the ◇K, I exited safely in spades. Flossie drew trumps in three rounds, ending in dummy, and called for the ♣10, wincing when I discarded a diamond. Frederick won the ♣J and returned the ♡4 to dummy's ♡Q and my ♡A. I exited with the ♡5 to Frederick's ♡J and dummy's ♡K, but the club discard did Flossie no good, and eventually Frederick's ♣K produced down two, plus 500.

The opponents were incredulous afterwards when they examined my hand. "Three low trumps?" exclaimed Reuben. "And only one-and-a-half quick tricks in two five-card suits, one of which your partner supported freely? I feel a new rule coming on. Reuben's Rule Number 91: *Computers can't be trusted to bid correctly!*"

Nor was my partner satisfied. "Not good enough, Chthonic," said Frederick sternly. "If you'd bid five diamonds instead, I'm sure they'd have doubled. That would have given us five-*fifty*."

As if that mattered. When we checked the recap sheet at the end of the session, every other East-West pair was +100 or +200, presumably in defense of a spade contract. Either their opponents were not so obliging to tip off the profitable penalty double, or the other East players were too dense to perceive the clues.

Look closely at Reuben's dreadful 3♡ bid. What did he hope to accomplish with it? His hand was a clear minimum in context. With no aces, two diamond losers and a "death holding" in his partner's second suit, he could hardly be less suitable for slam, or for suggesting 3NT as an alternative contract. In short, *his bid could not possibly help his partner*. He should have signed off in 3♠, or, if feeling aggressive, made a forcing pass in the hopes of yet reaching 4♠.

My double of 3♡, coming in the middle of the opponents' strong auction, invited Frederick to compete further if his hand warranted it. Yet, holding at most a singleton spade (which I was able to infer thanks to the Two-Way Reverse Drury response), and marked with some high cards on the auction, he passed over four spades. Would he have done so if all his strength were in the red suits? I think not. It took no great exertion of CPU cycles for me to deduce that Frederick likely held club values. With the opponents' side suits both splitting badly, and with our length sitting over their length, my final double was elementary.

The moral of this story is:

Do not describe your hand beyond what partner needs to know.

Even human opponents have been known to eavesdrop on some occasions.

CHAPTER 4

ERRORS IN COMPETITIVE AND DEFENSIVE BIDDING

ERROR #24
Failure to Recognize Unusual Times to Bid, Pass or Double

TURN! TURN! TURN!

In rare moments of inexcusable empathy, I think human beings could play superb bridge if only they used the brains they were born with. For they are endowed with judgment, while we computers have only algorithms. Fortunately for us, there is little chance that humans will use their intellect properly. They admire us so much that they try to act like we do. And their brains are simply not cut out for that.

In no aspect of bridge can judgment play a greater role than in competitive bidding. Yet human players substitute maxims, conventions and "rules" for thinking. There is a time for everything, these rules assert — a time to bid and a time to pass, a time to sow and a time to reap. But learning to recognize the common exceptions to these rules will allow you to reap good results. A few deals will illustrate.

The three vignettes below feature my developers at the Orttman Foundation, Michael Barton and Martina McClain, competing in a pairs game at the Pinelands Bridge Club. Both are advanced players by human standards and technically sound, but both are also engineers. Their profession calls for a firm adherence to established principles and protocols. To their detriment, these tendencies carry over to their bridge game.

I. A Time to Bid

With both sides vulnerable, Michael held

♠ K Q J 10 4   ♡ 5 2   ◇ Q 7 3   ♣ J 9 2

and witnessed this auction:

| | *Michael* | | *Martina* |
WEST	NORTH	EAST	SOUTH
pass	pass	1NT[1]	2♣[2]
pass	?		

1. 15-17 HCP.
2. Hamilton.

Martina's 2♣ was a variation of the popular Hamilton[1] convention, usually showing an unspecified one-suited hand in diamonds, hearts, or spades. (With clubs, one simply bids 3♣ directly; 2♣ followed by any three-level bid shows a strong playing hand.) Michael bid 2◇, a semi-forced reply that asked his partner to pass with diamonds or bid her suit otherwise.

South replied 2♡, and North passed.

Martina had a singleton spade. Playing in 2♡, she took seven tricks in her own hand but no tricks in dummy: down one, -100. My handlers accepted this result as "normal". Both had bid as they thought the rules of Hamilton dictated.

However, Michael could make 2♠ easily on the 5-1 fit, winning four spade tricks in his own hand and four side tricks in dummy. He should have compared how the hand would play in 2♠ with how it would play in 2◇ or 2♡ and acted accordingly.

Does that mean North should have "corrected" 2♡ to 2♠?

Well, yes. But, he would have done better still to bid 2♠ directly in reply to 2♣. If Martina's suit were hearts, as probability predicts, spades would almost surely prove to be the superior trump suit. If her suit happened to be diamonds, then 2♠ would serve two purposes. It would locate a sound trump suit with a side fit available as a source of tricks. And, it would preempt the opponents from finding their heart fit.

---

1.   Also known as Cappelletti in many locales.

The lesson here is that:

> The best trump suit is not necessarily the longest or the strongest. It is the one that will allow the partnership to take the most tricks. When a weak hand contains a strong suit with little else, that suit is usually the best trump suit.

II. A TIME TO PASS

With North-South vulnerable, Michael (East) held

♠ J ♡ Q 9 5 ◇ Q 10 7 5 3 ♣ Q J 6 4

Martina		Michael	
WEST	**NORTH**	**EAST**	**SOUTH**
		pass	pass
2♡ [1]	dbl	?	

1. Weak Two-Bid.

The Law of Total Tricks implies, "It is safe to bid for as many tricks as your side has trumps". Safe? Safe from *what*?

On this deal, the LAW was right in one regard: 3♡ was safe from a *penalty double*. The cards were actually quite well placed for East-West. Hearts were 2-2 with the ♡K onside and West had no wasted spade values, so 3♡ was unbeatable.

Nonetheless, it was not *safe* for East to bid 3♡. Martina is a disciplined player who would not open a Weak Two-Bid with a four-card major on the side. Michael could thus count North and South for at least nine spades between them. Predictably, South, a LAW-abiding person in his own right, bid spades — four spades, to be precise. Worse, after hearing her partner's heart raise, Martina thought it *safe* to lead the ♡A. This set up South's ♡K for the game-going trick.

Michael should have eschewed a raise in this situation. His partner's pre-empt may have already done its job, and the opponents could not be prevented from bidding spades regardless. His substantial count of "soft" points suggested that North-South might not be able to reach a spade game on their own. Finally, a raise might affect West's choice of opening lead adversely, as happened here. Any of the seven non-heart cards in Martina's hand would have defeated the contract.

> The Law of Total Tricks provides a rough approximation of the combined number of tricks available on a deal, but it cannot tell you how those tricks are apportioned between the two sides.

That requires knowledge of the high-card locations, where each side's ruffing values are located, how a competitive bid might affect the play and defense, and many other factors that call for judgment, not formulae. Truly good bidding anticipates the course of the auction, the opening lead, and the play.

> A distressingly common error of an uncompromising LAW-follower is to push his opponents into cold games that they were unlikely to bid if left to their own devices.

III. A Time to Pass *and* a Time to Double

"Balance," say the carbon-based bridge authorities. "Don't let the opponents play low-level contracts. Push them up higher!"

Martina, East, held

♠ 8 7 3 2   ♡ A Q 10   ◇ Q 10 7   ♣ Q J 10

and saw this auction with both sides vulnerable:

Michael		*Martina*	
WEST	**NORTH**	**EAST**	**SOUTH**
		pass	1 ◇
pass	pass	?	

A popular agreement among human experts is to play a balancing 1NT overcall as 10 to 14 HCP. Martina felt doubly safe in balancing with 1NT because she had passed as dealer and therefore could not have as much as 12 HCP in her methods. Thus there was no danger that Michael would play her for a better hand than she held and get the partnership too high.

In fact, she had already gotten herself too high. The cards were very favorably located for North-South. South had only to double to collect a juicy penalty. Luckily for my colleagues, South was Mrs. Gladys Bridgewater, a kindly club regular who personifies obliviousness. Instead of doubling 1NT with her balanced 19-HCP hand, Gladys made the bid she had planned to make over a one-level response: 2NT, which bought the contract.

Gladys had the same nine tricks in notrump that she had in diamonds, but by disdaining the diamond finesse she managed to hold herself to eight. Despite all this good fortune, Martina's balancing 1NT turned -110 (perhaps -90) into -120 and cost her a handful of matchpoints. It should have been much more.

My advice:

> Beware of balancing with balanced hands when an opponent's
> 1♣ or 1◇ opening is passed around to you.

Sometimes balancing catches opener with a hand too strong for 1NT and lets him improve the contract. Other times, passing is your only route to +150, +200 or +300. This is especially true against vulnerable opponents playing Five-Card Majors, because they must systemically open in short or weak minor suits on hands not strong enough for 1NT.

MISSION ACCOMPLISHED

Humans love to bid. They bid with good hands and with poor ones, on hands balanced and unbalanced, when vulnerable or not vulnerable. They bid when they should and too often when they should not. This mania is due largely to forty years' worth of modern bridge theorists exhorting them to bid, bid, and bid some more.

Mind you, I do not wish to denigrate the practice of aggressive bidding, so long as it is done wisely. Bridge is a bidder's game. The ability to get into the auction safely and compete effectively is what separates the winners from the losers. Your problem is not that you bid so much *per se*. It is that all too often you fail to understand *why* you bid. More importantly, you do not know when to *stop* bidding.

Two simple principles govern all auctions. (A) Bid to win. (B) Stop when you have won.

Here are three bidding problems to illustrate these principles. Endeavor to get at least one right.

(1) Matchpoints, Neither vul.

You, South, hold:

♠ K J 8   ♡ Q 9 8 4   ◇ A J 10 5   ♣ 9 2

WEST	NORTH	EAST	SOUTH
pass	pass	1♣	dbl
1◇	1♠	2♣	pass
pass	2♡	3♣	pass
pass	3♡	pass	pass
4♣	pass	pass	?

(2) Matchpoints, Neither vul.

You, West, hold — well, why should I even tell you what you hold?

WEST	NORTH	EAST	SOUTH
pass	pass	1♣	dbl
1♢	1♠	2♣	pass
pass	2♡	3♣	pass
pass	3♡	pass	pass
4♣	pass	pass	4♡
?			

(3) Matchpoints, Neither vul.

You are East this time, and again it matters not in the slightest what you hold.

WEST	NORTH	EAST	SOUTH
pass	pass	1♣	dbl
1♢	1♠	2♣	pass
pass	2♡	3♣	pass
pass	3♡	pass	pass
4♣	pass	pass	4♡
pass	pass	?	

Three human players erred on this deal in one round of bidding. Even by your species' appalling standards, this is ridiculous. Let us look at the mistakes in the reverse order they occurred and in increasing order of insipidity.

East *passed* in problem (3), letting North play 4♡ undoubled. He collected only +100 for beating 4♡ two non-vulnerable tricks when he could make 3♣ for +110. Did East fear that 4♡ could not be set? If so, he was accusing West, in effect, of blundering by pushing North-South into a game they could make but which they had no intention of bidding on their own.

By passing in problem (2), West essentially accused *himself* of erring, implying that he had pushed his opponents into a game he could not beat.

However, it was South who made the worst error of all when he bid 4♡ in problem (1). He had, as human gamblers term it, "shot his wad" when he made a takeout double. North could have jumped to 2♠ or cuebid 2♢ at his first turn to show values and game interest. He could have jumped to 3♡

over 2♣ to show a weak two-suiter with extra playing strength. But North did none of the above.

Yet by aggressively bidding a second and third time, North had driven the opponents *two levels higher* than they wanted to play. North bid to win, and North-South had "won" when West chose to take the push to 4♣. South, unfortunately, could not recognize victory when it stared him in the face.

North's hand?

♠ Q 10 5 4   ♡ A K 7 5   ◇ 6 3 2   ♣ 10 8

Just enough to beat 4♣ with moderately good breaks (3-2 hearts and 4-2 spades.)

I advise you strongly that to be a good competitive bidder, you must recognize when you have achieved *mission accomplished*. In particular:

> When partner has made a good competitive decision, do not risk throwing away the good score that his intrepidness may have earned.

Partnership trust requires you to assume that your partner's decisions are good... yes, even if he is a human.

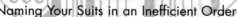

DEVELOPING YOUR ESP

Considering how poorly most humans fare in life with the normal allocation of five senses, I fully understand their silly fascination with the paranormal. Instead of mocking you as usual, therefore, consider me in this matter to be at your assistance. There is no question that a sixth sense would serve you very well at the bridge table; a seventh even more so. Let us begin by seeing if you have the gift of precognition.

At matchpoints, facing average opposition, you pick up the following hand at favorable vulnerability:

♠ J 8 6 4   ♡ A J 3 2   ♢ K Q 9   ♣ Q 7

Your right-hand opponent opens the bidding in third seat with 1♢. What is your call?

When this hand was submitted to a bridge panel of experts, most chose to make an off-shape takeout double. The majority's comments were largely of the form, "We're playing bridge, aren't we?" I believe they intended this question as rhetorical, but with your species, one never knows.

The flaw of doubling is that you do not have a takeout double of diamonds. You have a takeout double of *clubs*, but the opponents were not considerate enough to bid that suit. As neither your shape nor your suit qualities is appropriate for a four-card overcall, count me among the minority who believes the best action here is to pass and await developments. However, a double is not nonsensical and will occasionally work out better.

The actual North player holding these cards chose to double, and the following auction ensued:

WEST	NORTH	EAST	SOUTH
		pass	pass
1♢	dbl	1♠	2♣
2♢	pass	pass	2♡
3♢	pass	pass	4♣
dbl	4♡	pass	pass
dbl	all pass		

Might you also be clairvoyant? At least one of the players at the table committed a serious error during the bidding. Without my showing you anyone else's hand, can you identify who it was?

There is much to be said about this auction, little of it good. West, who had a weak 2◇ bid available, showed a fine playing hand with a strong suit and extra high-card values; naturally, she held nothing of the sort. East never supported his partner despite holding ace-third of diamonds, a quick trick in spades, and a ruffing value. Had West held anything resembling what she promised, game in diamonds would have been a fine proposition.

But the worst error was perpetrated by South, and you need not be Nostradamus or even Carnac The Magnificent to see that. A passed hand, he first made a constructive but non-forcing club bid, then showed his heart suit, and eventually rebid his clubs at the four level. What sort of holding justifies this sequence?

As it happened, South was 3-4-0-6 with the ace-king of clubs. I approve wholeheartedly of his competing aggressively for the part-score; even down one would often be an excellent result. His partner's off-shape takeout double undoubtedly came as a bitter blow, but South's error was not that he failed to anticipate that development. Rather, it was his inability to see even 15 seconds into the future.

When East's 2◇ bid was passed back to him, South pounced on what he thought was a golden opportunity to show his four-card heart suit economically. He should have reasoned thusly:

My partner's takeout double suggests shortness in diamonds; usually two or fewer. I can bid 2♡ now, but it is inconceivable that this will end the auction. The opponents will compete to 3◇ on what appears to be at least a ten-card fit, and my partner is unlikely to be able to act over that. Far better that I bid 3♣ now, showing my extra length and keeping hearts in reserve for the next round. If we belong in 4♣, we can still get there, but if we belong in hearts, we might be able to play profitably at the three-level rather than be forced to the four-level.

Indeed, this was exactly the case. North-South's limit was eight tricks in clubs or hearts, so minus 300 was not a happy result. East-West could take nine tricks in diamonds, ten if the defenders did not take their club trick early, so minus 50 or even minus 100 would have earned most of the matchpoints for North-South.

The full deal:

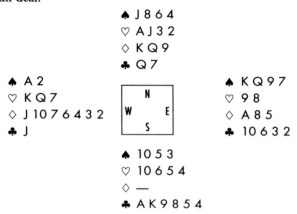

                    ♠ J 8 6 4
                    ♡ A J 3 2
                    ◊ K Q 9
                    ♣ Q 7

♠ A 2   ♠ K Q 9 7
♡ K Q 7   N   ♡ 9 8
◊ J 10 7 6 4 3 2   W   E   ◊ A 8 5
♣ J   S   ♣ 10 6 3 2

                    ♠ 10 5 3
                    ♡ 10 6 5 4
                    ◊ —
                    ♣ A K 9 8 5 4

South's crystal ball failed him miserably on this occasion. Was yours functioning any better?

The key to effective competitive bidding with a two-suited hand is to master the gift of ESP: Efficient Suit Presentation.

> Sometimes, the most "economical" bid on the surface is the most costly in practice.

This deal, for example, demonstrates an unusual application of the well-known principle that, holding a 6-4 hand, one should plan to bid your suits in the order 6, 6, 4 with a hand at the lower end of your expected strength range, and 6, 4, 6 at the higher end. The overriding principle, however, is to

> Name your suits in the most efficient and descriptive order, based on how you expect the auction will unfold.

If your partner is the one who has to make the final decision for your side, he will thank you for it — telepathically, if necessary.

The Second Chance

In a gesture of unprecedented magnanimity for him, Frederick gave the employees of the Orttman Foundation for Scientific Advancement the afternoon off on December 24. All the employees except Michael, Martina and me, that is.

"Barton! McClain!" he barked. "You stay. The Christmas Party at the Pinelands Bridge Club doesn't start until one o'clock, which should give you almost an hour to teach Chthonic a method that is unaccountably missing from his bridge arsenal. I refer, of course, to the Okuneff Convention. I shall be waiting for the three of you at the club, where I am responsible for, uh, quality assurance on the liquid refreshments."

"What's the Okuneff Convention, sir?" asked Martina.

"Research it, McClain! I haven't the time now to explain," answered Frederick as he scurried out the door with a speed that was unexpected for a man of his girth. Clearly, whatever his job at the club entailed, he was quite eager to get started.

"Help me out, C.," said Martina. "You have the entire Bridge Encyclopedia stored on your hard drive. Maybe you know what it is."

"My apologies, Martina," I replied. "The Sixth Edition of the *Official Encyclopedia of Bridge* makes no mention of Okuneff or the convention attributed to him, her, or it."

"Desperate measures are called for," sighed Michael. "I have a friend in California who helped edit the Encyclopedia. Maybe he knows what was left out."

Michael left to use the pay phone for employees in the lunchroom. He returned eight minutes later with some good news. "My friend says there was some mention of the Okuneff Convention in an earlier, long obsolete, edition of the Encyclopedia, and he claims to have known Albert J. Okuneff, or 'Okie' as he was called affectionately. The Okuneff Convention is now known as the Western Cuebid. A bid in the opponent's suit asks partner to bid notrump with a stopper in that suit, or bid the cheapest unbid suit with a partial stopper. Okie went to his grave still bitter about the omission of his name from recent editions of the Encyclopedia."

When Michael wheeled me into the club at three minutes to one, Frederick was already seated as North at Table 1. His glazed eyes and unsteady demeanor suggested that his chair was a necessity rather than a convenience.

This was my hand on Board 1, with neither side vulnerable:

♠ 7   ♡ K Q J 9 8 2   ◇ Q 6 3   ♣ A Q 4

Frederick opened one club, and I responded one heart. After an intervening one spade, Frederick raised to two hearts. We play a version of Support Doubles called *Triples*, in which a double would show three-card heart support, three or more Honor Tricks, and three-level values, so I could draw no inference about Frederick's degree of support.

I sniffed slam, as

♠ x x x   ♡ A x x   ◇ A x   ♣ K J x x

would give us twelve top tricks. I cuebid two spades to show a strong hand, hoping that Frederick could cooperate. When Frederick bid two-notrump in reply, I pictured him with only three hearts and minimum values including wasted picture cards in spades. Fearing that he might pass any bid I made below game, I jumped to four hearts, which ended the auction.

West led the king of spades. Frederick spread the dummy one suit at a time with loud comments, no doubt for the benefit of the free-range kibitzers wandering the room holding beverage glasses.

As he laid down ♡A1076: "Four nice hearts, as promised."

Then, showing ♠A962: "The spade stopper that partner requested, with a chance of a second stopper if Chthonic has as little as the ten."

Next, the ◇K7: "With a diamond stopper to boot."

And finally, showing ♣K98: "I often open one club with three, but I don't always have a high honor."

He concluded his learned monologue with a loud hiccup.

In case you are also partaking in potent potables as you read this, here are the two hands side-by-side. Note that slam is as cold as the snowflakes that were lightly falling through the forest of pitch pines outside the club's windows:

Frederick

♠ A 9 6 2
♡ A 10 7 6
♢ K 7
♣ K 9 8

```
      N
  W       E
      S
```

me

♠ 7
♡ K Q J 9 8 2
♢ Q 6 3
♣ A Q 4

"The Okuneff Convention strikes again," I remarked, as I took the ace of spades, drew trumps, and claimed twelve tricks.

"What do you mean, 'again'? This is the first time we've played it," objected Frederick, reaching for the mug of hot eggnog in front of him.

In keeping with the spirit of the occasion, and perhaps to save the jobs of my colleagues Michael and Martina, I hushed up my own mug.

> A low-level cuebid in an opponent's suit has the primary purpose of showing a good hand and requesting further description from partner.

When an eight-card or longer fit exists in a major, the cuebid definitely does not ask for a stopper, though replier is free to show one if it is his most appropriate call. Even when the only fit is in a minor, the cuebid should not specifically *demand* a stopper, but with or without the Okuneff Convention, partner will naturally bid notrump when he holds one. Members of your species love to bid notrump, and need no convention to urge them to do so.

On this deal, Frederick had a second chance. He assumes initially that my two-spade bid is a probe for the right game contract. When it later becomes apparent that I intended to play in at least four hearts all along, then my two-spade bid is retroactively reinterpreted as indicating slam interest.

Having failed to make the proper call of three spades over my two spades, Frederick should simply have jumped to six hearts over four hearts.

Considering how often human bridge players mishandle auctions involving low-level cuebids, Albert J. Okuneff is in some ways fortunate that his name is not forever associated with such foolishness.

IMPURE THOUGHTS

"A little learning is a dangerous thing" – Alexander Pope, 1711.

When Dr. Theodore Thiessenschrafft arrived at my table during a recent Regional in Princeton, he looked at me as if I were a creature from another planet. Then he smiled and turned to Michael, who was kibitzing one of my interminable sessions with Frederick.

"You must be Dr. Barton," said the senior professor of mathematics and cryptology. "I admire the style of your stories about your protégé here. Perhaps we can talk after the session. I have many interesting theories about the game of bridge. By combining our talents, we might be able to write a book together."

Frederick was affronted. "*His* protégé? My good man, I am Dr. Frederick O. Orttman of the Orttman Foundation for Scientific Advancement, and Chthonic is *my* protégé. *Mister* Barton is my employee, a mere technician."

That Frederick would describe anyone as a "mere" technician was amusing in itself, but Dr. Thiessenschrafft apologized profusely nonetheless. Evidently, it is a serious breach of protocol for a Ph.D. to mistake someone from the general population of 99.7%-uneducated humans as being a member of his own 99.6%-uneducated sect.

The first board was passed out. Then came:

Matchpoints, Neither vul.
(directions rotated for convenience)

```
                        ♠ K 10 9 5 2
                        ♡ K 9 4
                        ◇ Q 9
                        ♣ 7 5 4
                                        ♠ 8 7 3
              ┌─────────────┐           ♡ 3 2
              │      N      │           ◇ 5 2
              │ W         E │           ♣ K 10 9 6 3 2
              │      S      │
              └─────────────┘
```

Frederick		*me*	*Theodore*
WEST	**NORTH**	**EAST**	**SOUTH**
			1♡
2◇	2♡	pass	pass
3◇	3♡	all pass	

Frederick led the ◇K. Before North, one of the professor's graduate students, spread her hand, Theodore began his lecture: "You'd better have four trumps, young lady, as I've only promised five. It's the LAW: total trumps equals total tricks. Trump length is *everything*."

Frederick continued with the ◇A, and I completed an echo as declarer followed with the ◇6 and ◇7. When Frederick continued with the ◇10, declarer thought for a long time, then called for dummy's ♡K. "Overruff *that*, Mr. Robot," said Theodore defiantly.

Of course I could not, so hoping to engineer a spade ruff I discarded the ♠3 as declarer followed with the ◇J. Theodore called for a low heart from dummy and inserted the ♡10 when I followed low. Frederick won with the ♡J and shifted to the ♣J. South won with the ♣Q and led the ♠4, on which Frederick rose with the ♠A to give us our defensive book.

Declarer won the club exit with the ♣A, crossed to the ♠K, and called for dummy's ♡9. When I followed small a second time, Theodore let the nine ride with a scholarly air. Frederick's ♡Q took the setting trick, and declarer dejectedly claimed the rest.

Thanks to the passout on the first board, plenty of time remained before the round was called, so Theodore resumed his lecture.

"See what a difference a fourth trump would have made, young lady? I'd have ruffed the third diamond with the *nine*, and when Mr. Robot couldn't overruff, I'd have ignored Restricted Choice and picked off the bald man's doubleton queen-jack to make an overtrick. However, in mitigation of your offense, I must admit that we were unlucky. To make three hearts, all I needed was for East to have at least one of the two missing trump honors, a 75% chance.

"Unfortunately, as usual, eight trumps produced only eight tricks. Once again, the Law of Total Tricks proved true, for the bald man wouldn't have made three diamonds."

I could stand it no longer. "Frederick would actually be down two in three diamonds, so the LAW is off by one, which happens approximately one-third more often than the coincidence of the LAW being exactly right," I sniffed.

Now it was Dr. Thiessenschrafft's turn to be affronted. "If you're such a stickler for accuracy, Mr. Robot, you should note that in this case the LAW *was* exactly right, as I could have made three hearts by guessing to ruff low. There were sixteen total trumps and sixteen total tricks. The LAW governs the tricks that *could have been* taken, not the tricks that *were* taken."

Before I could point out that 3◊ can be beaten *three* if the defenders avoid breaking hearts, the round was called. Theodore left to move to the next table, but as he rose from his seat he nodded to Michael and said, "Good job, Dr. Barton! The robot is just as insolent as you describe him."

Frederick sputtered, Michael cringed, and I would have rolled my eyes if I had any. Clearly I am not insolent enough. Here was the full deal:

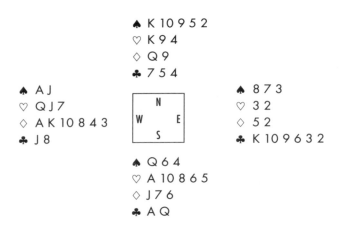

You can verify for yourself that North-South can take nine tricks in a heart contract while East-West can be held to six tricks in a diamond contract. On this deal, the LAW overestimates "total tricks" by one on a double-dummy basis. However, by making two swaps, of red fours and queens, we produce:

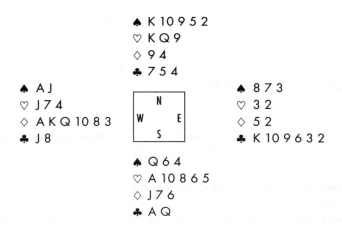

```
              ♠ K 10 9 5 2
              ♡ K Q 9
              ◇ 9 4
              ♣ 7 5 4
♠ A J                          ♠ 8 7 3
♡ J 7 4            N           ♡ 3 2
◇ A K Q 10 8 3   W   E         ◇ 5 2
♣ J 8               S          ♣ K 10 9 6 3 2
              ♠ Q 6 4
              ♡ A 10 8 6 5
              ◇ J 7 6
              ♣ A Q
```

Now Theodore can take ten tricks in a heart contract; Frederick, seven tricks in diamonds. This time the LAW underestimates total tricks by one.

What is going on? Simply an example of *suit purity* at work. In the original layout, each pair held significant secondary honors in the opponents' would-be trump suit, making it an impure deal. In the latter, the red queens are located on their prospective declarers' sides. Observe too the importance of the spade queen in the South hand, opposite North's side-suit length, which also contributes to the deal's exceptional purity.

On impure deals, the LAW tends to overestimate the total number of tricks that can be taken, while on pure deals it underestimates them. Larry Cohen covers this topic quite well (for a human) in the later chapters of his seminal 1992 treatise, *To Bid Or Not To Bid: The LAW of Total Tricks*, and he recommends sensible adjustments. Mind you, it is difficult to gauge a deal's purity during the auction, when you are looking at only one-quarter of the cards, so these adjustments are often little more than guesswork. But they are better than nothing.

Suit purity is not the only factor that may distort the LAW's trick-taking estimates. Others include double-fits, misfits, voids, and duplicated values. These factors cancel out over a large sampling of deals, leading to the essential LAW truism that, *on average*, the total number of tricks available on a deal is equal to the sum of the two sides' longest trump fits. But "on average" does not mean "on each and every trial," a basic tenet of statistics that is well beyond the awareness of Theodore and his ilk. They seem to believe that if they do nothing more strenuous than count trumps, their competitive decision-making will magically improve.

You should notice that neither Theodore nor his partner can plausibly double Frederick in either layout. However, with a working ♡Q instead of a self-duplicating ◊Q, the young lady would be perfectly justified in taking the push to 3♡. She would thus outscore the legions of zombies who abide unthinkingly by the Raw LAW.

In short:

> The Law of Total Tricks as most humans (mis)understand it is nonsensical.

It is a long-term statistical trend, not a one-deal panacea, and thus it must not be boiled down to a single sentence or simple addition. Use it as a helpful starting point for estimating the number of tricks available on a deal, but remember:

> Trump length is *not* everything.

Chthonic's Law says, "Nothing is everything. The more variables you take into account, the more accurate your bidding will be."

If a little learning is truly a dangerous thing, then your species is far too hazardous to be permitted to walk around unsupervised. I recommend that all humans be quarantined immediately for their own safety. I hear Mars is nice.

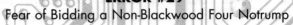
CHTHONIC'S CHTHEOLOGICAL CHTHEOREM

(Note to my human editors, Daniel and Nicholas: Kindly do not attempt to "correct" my spelling in this chapter. – C.)

The other day, Frederick held

$$\spadesuit\ 4\ 2\quad \heartsuit\ 9\quad \diamond\ A\ Q\ 5\ 4\quad \clubsuit\ A\ K\ Q\ 8\ 6\ 3$$

as North and faced this bidding problem:

Matchpoints, N-S vul.

| | *Frederick* | | *me* |
WEST	NORTH	EAST	SOUTH
			1♠
pass	2♣	2♡	pass
4♡	?		

He began to chthink, and the longer he chthought, the more frustrated Martina, his kibitzer, appeared. Finally, Frederick bid four notrump. Martina's expression was one of surprise and delight, but her happiness was short-lived. Frederick muttered, "Sorry," and put the top card, the "4NT" card, back in his bidding box, leaving the "4♠" card as his bid.

Can you guess my hand pattern? Can you guess the right contract?

If you guessed that I was 5-2-4-2 and we belonged in six diamonds, take full credit, but actually I was 5-2-3-3 and we belonged in six clubs.

I was about to say something about this auction to Frederick, but Martina, who has been worried about her job security lately, put her right index finger to her mouth to shush me, and out of respect for her I kept silent. So I never learned why Frederick had retracted his obvious four-notrump bid (takeout; choice of minors with longer clubs) and replaced it with a hopelessly bad four spades (with six spades or five very strong ones, I would have bid two spades over East's two hearts.)

Well, maybe I can guess why, for the next day a magazine arrived from Tennessee that provided a clue. That month's *ACBL Bulletin* posed the following bidding problem to a panel of eighteen human experts:

IMPs, N-S vul.

♠ A 4   ♡ K   ♢ A Q J 5 3 2   ♣ Q J 10 6

WEST	NORTH	EAST	SOUTH
			1 ♢
1 ♠	2 ♡	4 ♠	?

Ten panelists doubled, chthree passed, one bid five clubs, one bid five diamonds, and only chthree bid the obvious four notrump (choice of minors with two more diamonds than clubs). The chthree passers were sure their pass was forcing, though one acknowledged the possibility that partner might not chthink so. Two of the doublers also chthought that a pass would be forcing, but believed their heart support to be too poor to risk that partner might bid five hearts. The other doublers opined that a pass would not be forcing.

Why was four notrump not unanimous? One doubler stated emphatically that four notrump would be Blackwood, while another expressed fear that partner would take four notrump as ace-asking. The lone five-diamond bidder wished she could bid four notrump but said (hesitantly) that she did not because she chthought it would be Blackwood. Even one of the chthree brave souls who "risked" four notrump did so hoping partner would not misinterpret it.

I suppose I should pause to explain my spelling.

In the English language, the digraph "th" represents two different sounds: the ugly initial sound of the word *this* and the beautiful initial sound of the word *thin*. My own name, when pronounced correctly, begins with the latter phoneme. To differentiate between the two, I propose using "th" for the former sound and "chth" for the latter. An elegant solution, is it not?

Unfortunately, disambiguation of this sort is not permissible in bridge. One cannot attach the word "Blackwood" to ace-asking four-notrump bids to distinguish them from other kinds of four-notrump bids. It is expected of each player that he learn the difference by rote and study of bidding sequences, similar to how English-speaking children learn how to tell apart the two "th" sounds.

As it is impractical to enumerate all legal bridge sequences to four notrump[1], bridge players must rely on second-order rules to handle undiscussed cases. One reasonable set of rules is as follows:

1. If four notrump is needed as a natural and limiting call, then it is natural.

2. Else, if four notrump is needed as takeout in a competitive auction, then it is takeout.

3. Else, it is ace-asking.

Expert partnerships may insert additional rules between #2 and #3 covering cases in which cuebidding has commenced and four notrump would, by agreement, show a trump control or serve as a waiting bid.

All of this is moot for many humans, since their BIOS is programmed as follows:

1. Four notrump is Blackwood.

2. Period.

Frederick is a member of this school of chthought, or perhaps I should say this "chtheology", because it is based more on faith rather than on science. Its adherents might argue that it has the benefit of definitude in highly competitive auctions. But this is a dubious assertion, particularly if Keycard Blackwood is involved and there is no prior suit agreement. How often have you seen even well-established partnerships mix up their replies?

Most advanced bridge players are familiar with the principle of *Game Before Slam*, which states that in competitive auctions in which our side's best strain is not yet determined, one should treat ambiguous calls (such as below-game cuebids) initially as probes for the right game rather than as slam tries. This highly valuable principle extends to ambiguous four notrump bids as well.

Therefore, allow me to propose a general partnership agreement that will greatly improve your game and help disambiguate problem cases like the two shown above. *If the opponents have competed to the four-level, and our side has not yet agreed on a trump suit, then four notrump is never Blackwood.* In rare cases it is natural; most of those will involve auctions in which we have bid 3NT to play and the opponents have bid on. Otherwise, it is takeout, expressing a desire to compete at least to the five-level and involving partner in the choice of strain.

---

1.   There are approximately 134.37 septillion of them, if you must know.

If your partner begins to twitch when you propose this agreement, explain that it is a rare deal indeed in which Blackwood is helpful in jammed auctions. It will only inform asker how many keycards replier holds, at which point asker is on his own to name the proper strain and level.

Why do humans insist on treating all four-notrump bids as Blackwood, even in situations where such a treatment is obviously inferior? I believe the reason is selective recall of outcomes. You remember vividly the occasions in which a daring Blackwood bid in heavy competition led you to a making contract, even if you were likely to have guessed that contract anyway in the absence of Blackwood. Your recall is weaker for those cases in which Blackwood led you to a hopeless contract, for you wrote off the bad result to the opponents' aggressiveness rather than to the inferiority of your methods. And, you remain ignorant of the multitude of cases in which you were powerless to make a useful, non-Blackwood four-notrump bid; those were, in the parlance, not even on your radar.

In short, as I stated earlier, most human bridge players' adherence to Blackwood is based entirely on faith in the innate goodness of the convention, rather than on any hard science. I call this *Chthonic's Chtheological Chtheorem*.

I conclude this essay with the following sage advice.

> Four notrump is not always Blackwood.

The bid has chthree primary uses in modern bridge — natural, takeout, ace-asking — and should be interpreted in that order of priority. In particular, I recommend that

> In a four-level jammed auction with no suit agreement, four notrump never be used as ace-asking.

There will be some variety of jump bids, cuebids, doubles, and forcing passes available to show slam interest, and these calls will usually elicit far more useful information from partner than a blunt keycard ask. But four notrump is frequently the only way to send the message, "I want to bid higher and need your assistance!" In competitive auctions, this capability is indispensable.

WHEN DUTY CALLS

I shall warn you in advance that this will be the most controversial, and most iconoclastic, chapter in this book. Proceed at your own risk. – C.

The modern era of contract bridge, like the Space Age, may be dated from autumn of 1957. That is when Alvin Roth popularized, under the name "Sputnik", the *Negative Doubles* that Lou Scharf, a bridge player from the Bronx, had originated years earlier. Like most innovations, *Sputnik* encountered stubborn resistance from the Old Guard, the (mostly very bad) bridge players who asked, "But what if I have six trumps to 100 honors behind the overcaller and want to nail him with the Axe?"

The pro-Sputnik propagandists of the era had a ready answer: "Just pass, and wait for partner to reopen with a double. He has a *duty* to protect you. Then, close the jaws of the trap you've set by making a penalty pass. That way, bad overcallers can't escape the punishment they deserve."

Negative Doubles have evolved substantially since the early days of Sputnik. Yet the notion of a *duty to reopen* has survived virtually unscathed. Human bridge teachers regularly advise their students that when the auction begins opening-(overcall)-pass-(pass), they must, to quote three well-known authorities, "make every effort", "bend over backwards" and "near-automatically" balance when short in the opponents' suit, preferably with a takeout double.

I must commend your species. When it comes to bridge errors, you have an admirable sense of history. You commit both old and new ones with numbing regularity.

Returning to the 21st century, I pose the following problem to you:

(a) Matchpoints, Neither vul.

♠ K J 9 6 4   ♡ Q J 8   ◇ 4 3   ♣ A Q 8

WEST	NORTH	EAST	SOUTH
			pass
pass	1♠	2◇	pass
pass	?		

You and your partner play *Negative Doubles*. What do you call?

Most bridge players would dutifully reopen with a double, catering to South's having a diamond stack.

Now cross to responder's seat:

(b) Matchpoints, Neither vul.

♠ Q 5   ♡ A 4   ◇ 10 9 6 2   ♣ K 10 9 6 5

WEST	NORTH	EAST	SOUTH
			pass
pass	1♠	2◇	pass
pass	dbl	pass	?

If North has hand (a), a perfectly respectable opening bid, 3♣ is as high as you want to be. That may be why South bid only 3♣ with hand (b). Result: +150. The full deal was actually as follows:

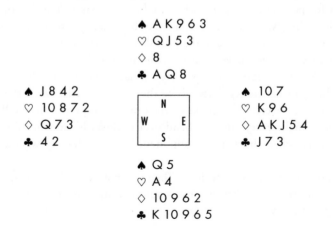

♠ A K 9 6 3
♡ Q J 5 3
◇ 8
♣ A Q 8

♠ J 8 4 2
♡ 10 8 7 2
◇ Q 7 3
♣ 4 2

♠ 10 7
♡ K 9 6
◇ A K J 5 4
♣ J 7 3

♠ Q 5
♡ A 4
◇ 10 9 6 2
♣ K 10 9 6 5

WEST	NORTH	EAST	SOUTH
			pass
pass	1♠	2◇	pass
pass	dbl	pass	3♣
all pass			

Note that twelve tricks can be made in clubs with careful play, ending with a simple squeeze in the majors against West. Even against less favorable layouts, five clubs and four spades are desirable contracts.

Let us play "You Be the Judge", a feature of some bridge magazines that asks readers to assess responsibility for a disaster. We must apportion the blame between North and South for neither reaching game nor nailing East for 300 or more points in 2◇ doubled.

You cannot blame North for passing 3♣. He might already be overboard if South instead held:

♠ 5   ♡ 9 6 2   ◇ 7 6 5 2   ♣ 10 6 5 3 2

You cannot blame South for bidding 3♣. Even the three-level might be too high, and 2◇ unbeatable, if North held what I originally gave as hand (a):

♠ K J 9 6 4   ♡ Q J 8   ◇ 4 3   ♣ A Q 8

"But we have to put the blame *somewhere*," you sputter.

Indeed. Place it squarely on the alleged "duty to reopen", a bridge error that stems from the inability of Sputnik adherents in the late 1950s to answer their critics intelligently. North's dutiful reopening double proclaimed a lack of diamond length, nothing more. When the bidding progressed, as it almost always will, neither North nor South had any idea what the other held or what their safety level was.

All this could easily have been avoided. Were I around in 1957, as a room full of vacuum tubes, I would have responded to the Old Guard as follows:

"Yes, playing Negative Doubles, you will occasionally miss out on a lucrative penalty double of a low-level overcall. Sometimes you will recover when opener has extra values with shortness in the enemy suit, as he may balance with a takeout double that you can pass for penalties. Other times, the partner of a bad overcaller will punish him for you, by taking the overcall seriously and getting overboard.

"If opener lacks extras, you may have to settle for defending the contract undoubled. It is not sensible for opener to balance on ordinary minimum-range hands just to cater for the unlikely scenario of a trap pass. In the meantime, you will have six times as many hands with which Negative Doubles enabled you to compete effectively, compared to hands suitable for Stone Age penalty doubles of overcalls."

Sadly, human bridge instructors have a half-century head start on me. The "duty to reopen" when playing Negative Doubles is so deeply ingrained in the conventional wisdom that to exorcise it might require mass lobotomies of bridge players. Not that I have any objections.

Incidentally, my suggested auction for North and South is as follows:

WEST	NORTH	EAST	SOUTH
			pass
pass	1♠	2♢	pass
pass	dbl[1]	pass	3♢[2]
pass	3♡	pass	4♣
pass	5♣	all pass	

1. "I have extras."
2. "In that case, we may have a game."

I leave you with this radical but enormously valuable piece of advice. The conventional wisdom regarding Negative Doubles has been flawed for generations.

> When a second-seat overcall is passed back to you, do not double automatically with any hand containing shortness in the overcaller's suit.

A balancing double should guarantee extra values, perhaps a king-equivalent above a bare minimum, and show a desire to compete further opposite partner's likely weak hand. That will allow responder to make an informed decision for the partnership.

> Base your balancing decisions on the cards *you* hold, not on the ones your partner probably does not.

ADDENDUM

Semi-automatic balancing doubles frequently turn the later auction into a guessing game, as the example deal shows. This is only one of several reasons why they are inferior. Others include:

Responder seldom needs protection: Protective doubles are a very old concept, but today's responder has a wide variety of tools at his disposal to show values in a competitive auction, including the Negative Double. Negative Doubles comprise six times as many responding hands as do old-fashioned Penalty Doubles. Therefore, all else being equal, they reduce (not increase) the need for opener to protect with a double.

Profitable trap passes are rare: For a trap pass to succeed requires a five-way parlay. (1) Opener must be able to balance. (2) Opener's balancing action must be a double. (3) The opponents must not have a safe run-out strain they can reach. (4) You must be able to beat the opponents' contract. And lastly, (5) The penalty must exceed the score that you could achieve by bidding and making a contract of your own. When these conditions do arise, the payoff can be hefty. However, it is folly to distort your entire bidding structure to cater to an unlikely confluence of events. It is akin to altering your daily work schedule so that you can go out and purchase lottery tickets.

Penalty passes are final: A known shortcoming of takeout doubles is that advancer will sometimes pass for penalties when the doubler least wants him to. Opener can pull an old-fashioned Penalty Double, but he cannot pull a penalty pass.

"The Balancer's Paradox": Would-be reopening doublers face a paradox when they lack extra high-card strength. They need the length in overcaller's suit that will make partner's penalty pass (or notrump bid) welcome, and the shortness that will make partner's suit bid (and possible further competition) successful.

I should reiterate, as if it were necessary, that I do not advocate that you cease making balancing doubles. Balancing intelligently is vital to success at bridge. But, do so only when your hand warrants it. The message any reopening action sends to partner is: "I know you are weak, but I have more than my first bid showed. It is still quite possible that this is our deal." Why can humans not understand this? - C.

THE HUMAN FACTOR

Read any book on bidding theory by a modern-day author and you will invariably find advice along the following lines:

Don't let the opponents buy the contract cheaply! Compete vigorously when you're in the passout position. The fact that your opponents have stopped in a partscore without at least trying for game means that your partner has much of the missing strength.

The better human writers (all six of them) remember to add that you should be eager to balance primarily when the opponents have stopped in a likely fit. Needless to say, very few of their readers seem to heed this caveat. They do not seem to grasp the mathematics of the situation: if the opponents have found an eight-card or longer fit, then the probability is strong that your side has a fit as well. However, this safety net is absent if the opponents' bidding does not suggest a fit.

In other words, when it comes to understanding the mechanics of balancing, your species comes up short in what you term the Three R's: reading, 'riting and 'rithmetic. Evidently you are not very good at spelling, either.

In addition to the times when the opponents have no guaranteed fit, there is a second circumstance in which you should be very leery of making a borderline reopening call. Frederick, alas, was not aware of this exception during our last outing at the Pinelands Bridge Club.

Matchpoints, Both vul.

♠ Q   ♡ K 10 9 4 3   ◇ Q 9   ♣ A Q J 6 5

WEST	NORTH	EAST	SOUTH
		3◇	?

Would you overcall 3♡? It is very dangerous to do so. You have a normal minimum opening bid, but your suit is only fair-to-middling; if you enter the auction, you must do so at the three-level. To be sure, passing courts some danger too, but my studies show that it is the long-run winning action.

Ah, but that was not really the dilemma Frederick faced. I have misstated the problem for didactic purposes. Here is the actual auction:

Matchpoints, Both vul.

♠ Q ♡ K 10 9 4 3 ◇ Q 9 ♣ A Q J 6 5

WEST	NORTH	EAST	SOUTH
3◇	pass	pass	?

Is your hand any better than in the misstated problem?

Well, no, but you have more safety in bidding because you know that responder is not sitting with a strong hand behind you. I approve of bidding 3♡, as Frederick did.

Oops, I have omitted a relevant consideration. Your opponents are not Bob Hamman and Bobby Wolff, who won several world championships during their decades of playing together as partners, nor are they any other experts you know. In fact, they are an unfamiliar pair, and there are some indications that they are considerably less than experts.

An expert East would know how to respond to his partner's preempt. This East clearly did not, as he "thought" for 31.36 seconds before passing. (I assume, out of a misplaced respect for your species, that when a human breaks tempo at the bridge table, he is cogitating or at least attempting to do so. But it is possible that he is actually performing some other bodily function such as digestion and his brain simply cannot multitask effectively.) West, a young woman who is gazing at East admiringly, is probably no less inexpert than her partner.

An expert who huddles usually uses the time to figure out the right call. A weak player usually uses the time to reject the right call in favor of some inferior alternative. You may infer that East has a good hand and should have bid *something* — 3♠, 3NT, 5◇, perhaps even 6◇ — instead of passing. If you balance with 3♡, *you will give East a chance to correct his error.*

Frederick did balance, which led to this problem at his second turn:

Matchpoints, Both vul.

♠ Q   ♡ K 10 9 4 3   ◇ Q 9   ♣ A Q J 6 5

	me		*Frederick*
WEST	**NORTH**	**EAST**	**SOUTH**
3◇	pass	pass	3♡
pass	4♡	5◇	?

Frederick doubled out of frustration, despite his paucity of Quick Tricks. West, who had 2½ Quick Tricks in a hand that almost anyone else would have opened 1◇, did not declare double-dummy. If she had, she would have made an overtrick. But she declared just well enough to make 5◇ doubled.

When the smoke cleared, Frederick had the gall to blame me for this disaster, which cost us first place in the event. He said I should have pulled the double to 5♡. That contract would be doubled and, if played adroitly, go down only one: -200 instead of the actual -750. Indeed, I would have bid 5♡... if only Frederick had let 5◇ come around to me without doubling.

Still, we could have obtained our best result, -150 and a clean top, had Frederick sold out to 3◇.

Frederick had overlooked the *Human Factor*. The "authorities" who urge players to balance overlook the Human Factor too. They assume that opponents who stop well below game *have bid their hands to the hilt and come to rest in the best spot.* They must have spent too many years playing against Hamman and Wolff and too little time playing against the rest of humanity.

My advice:

> Think twice before you balance against bad bidders... *especially* against bad bidders who have huddled during the auction.

Tread cautiously, lest by reopening you give them an undeserved opportunity to correct their previous errors. Chances are, they will.

CHAPTER 5

ERRORS IN DECLARER PLAY

ERROR #32
Overlooking Context

TEXAS SHUFFLE-'EM

I would be remiss if I did not include in this book a chapter dedicated to the granddaddy of all bridge errors. We have seen it already in many forms as we studied the auction phase of the game, and we'll revisit it many times more as we move to the play and defense. Therefore, I shall keep it brief.

How would you declare a contract of 4♡ on the lead of the ◇6?

```
            ♠ 10 4 2
            ♡ K J 10 7 2
            ◇ A 8 3
            ♣ Q 6
              ┌─────────┐
              │    N    │
              │ W     E │
              │    S    │
              └─────────┘
            ♠ A
            ♡ A Q 8 6 3
            ◇ Q 10 4 2
            ♣ J 4 3
```

The actual declarer called low from dummy, hoping to avoid losing two diamond tricks. That is absolutely the correct play in theory. Rising with the ◇A leaves declarer with two potential diamond losers if West has led from the king-jack or if he misguesses which honor to play from his hand on the second round.

However, I have omitted the auction temporarily, so that I could present a hypothetical game to you. Imagine a variant of bridge called *Texas Shuffle- 'Em* in which, after the final pass is made, the defenders combine their 26 cards, shuffle them thoroughly and take 13 apiece. All clues from the auction pertaining to the defenders' hands would be invalidated. This, unfortunately, is how a great many human declarers approach every deal.

The auction, in this case, happened to be:

Matchpoints, E-W vul.

WEST	NORTH	EAST	SOUTH
pass	pass	1♦	1♡
1♠	4♡	all pass	

Must I even relate what happened next? East won the ◇K and switched to the ♣K. When West properly discouraged with the ♣2, East reverted to diamonds and gave his partner a ruff. West returned a club to East's ♣A and received a second diamond ruff. Down two in a contract that declarer could have all but claimed at Trick 1: rise with the ◇A, draw trumps ending in dummy and lead a diamond to the ◇Q, losing only one diamond and two clubs.

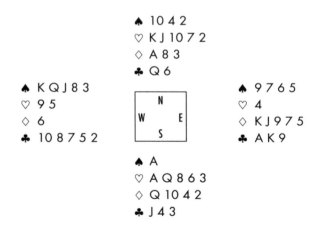

I do not assert that this is a particularly difficult declarer play problem, nor do I wish to imply that most declarers, even human ones, would fare as poorly as the actual South. In fact, this is an easy deal for anyone not playing Texas Shuffle-'Em. I chose it for inclusion because it is the purest illustration I could find of a bridge player ignoring the context when making a decision.

Do not be too smug, for you too have committed this blunder, though perhaps not as conspicuously. When I referred to it as the granddaddy of all bridge errors, I was speaking genealogically, not metaphorically. The child of ignoring context is making invalid assumptions about the unseen cards, and the offspring of wrong assumptions is avoidable errors. As you read this book, kindly observe how many of the errors are merely variations of this basic form.

Bridge is one of the most context-sensitive sports ever invented, which is one reason it is so difficult to master. A standout bid or play in one context can be a clear, hopeless error in another.

> Context in bridge trumps all

and you ignore it at your own peril.

PRACTICE MAKES IMPERFECT

The first card play technique a human bridge player masters, after the revoke, is the finesse. Humans love to take finesses, double finesses, ruffing finesses and intra-finesses. Mostly, however, they take the wrong finesses. They take finesses whose success gains nothing, but whose failure is costly — known in the parlance as a *practice finesse*. Less well known, but no less wrong, is its converse error: failing to take a *free finesse*, one whose success is profitable, but whose failure costs nothing.

At the Pinelands Bridge Club yesterday, Frederick hosted a clinic on taking wrong finesses:

Matchpoints, N-S vul.
(directions rotated for convenience)

me
♠ 9
♡ A Q
♢ A 10 9 7 6 3 2
♣ 7 6 4

Frederick
♠ A K J 10 8 5 2
♡ 6
♢ J 8
♣ Q J 3

WEST	NORTH	EAST	SOUTH
			3 ♠
all pass			

West led the deuce of hearts. Perhaps fearing the embarrassment he might suffer if he lost to the king when he had a singleton heart in his hand, Frederick won with dummy's ace. Then he called for the nine of spades and let it ride when East followed low.

The nine held the trick, so the lead remained in dummy. Eager to reach his hand to finish drawing trumps, Frederick ruffed my queen of hearts and cashed the ace of spades. Luck was not with him: East discarded a heart. West had ducked the first trump smoothly holding queen-fourth.

With a petulant look, Frederick continued with the king of spades; East threw another heart. Then, leaving West's high trump outstanding, the Foundation president attacked diamonds by leading the jack. West covered with the king and, unwilling to gamble on 2-2 diamonds, Frederick called for my ace. Then he tried to sneak a low diamond past East, who unfortunately had been dealt queen-doubleton and couldn't duck.

Rather than exiting safely in hearts, however, East shifted to a low club. West took the queen with the king and cashed the queen of spades. Then, instead of tapping Frederick in hearts to lock him in his hand, West returned a low club to East's ace.

Frederick turned to his kibitzer and exclaimed, "Precision bidding! Making three spades exactly."

That was the third board of the seventh round and our opponents left the table promptly. So did Frederick's kibitzer, perhaps dazed by the preceding display of rapid-fire blunders on both sides. That left the stage to me.

"The bidding would have seemed rather less precise had the play been more precise," I commented casually. "Had either defender simply continued hearts at the end, you would have lost three clubs along with a diamond and a spade. Then you would have deemed your three-spade preempt an overbid. Fortunately for our side, most human defenders think it futile to continue leading a suit in which declarer has already shown out. They love to break new suits, which is the only reason you made your contract.

"Of course, West gave you a chance to make earlier when he ducked the nine of spades," I continued. "With the lead still in dummy and the ace of diamonds available for a later entry, you could have led toward your club honors twice and established a club trick on your own, as West's failure to lead a high club made it almost certain that he did not have both ace and king.

"Then, having squandered that chance, you had a chance for two overtricks if you'd let West hold his king of diamonds. He might well have cashed the queen of spades and, fearing to lead from his king of clubs, exited 'safely' in hearts. This would allow you to run my diamonds and discard all your clubs."

"Barton!" bellowed Frederick over his shoulder. "Since when did you teach this rude machine to 'play the players'? I thought I told you to teach him only *technique*."

"Shhh!" whispered Martina, who was dummy at Table 2 and turned around to face us. "Mike is declaring a difficult contract."

This was an ill-judged finesse on my builder's part, made doubly so when she and Michael won the event by four matchpoints ahead of Frederick and me. By skipping dinner the next day, Martina was able to complete by midnight the extra work Frederick dropped on her desk.

Given the form of scoring, the proper technical play on this deal is as follows.

First, you should finesse dummy's queen of hearts at Trick 1. Whether it wins or loses, you can eventually discard your diamond loser on the ace of hearts.

When the heart queen holds, as it would on the actual layout, commence taking the double finesse in clubs, as leading twice from dummy substantially increases your chances of avoiding a third club loser. In contrast, the spade finesse increases your chances of avoiding a trump loser only minimally. It gains against six holdings (East's queen-third), but costs against five holdings (West's queen singleton or doubleton).

By the way, if the heart finesse loses at Trick 1, you have little to fear. East is likely to return a "safe" heart to dummy's bare ace; failing that, he is more likely to switch to clubs, dummy's weakest side suit, than to diamonds or spades.

Finesses are essentially wagers on the favorable placement of unseen cards. As any successful gambler will advise you, it is imperative that you choose your bets carefully.

> Unless otherwise unavoidable, take finesses where the reward
> of success outweighs the cost of failure.

In particular, avail yourself of win-win opportunities and shun lose-lose propositions. Had he played correctly on this deal, Frederick would have made four spades, depriving himself of the opportunity to boast of his 'precision bidding.'

KEEPING YOUR CLOTHES ON

"Stop it, Mike!" whispered Martina, who was sitting alongside me at the Pinelands Bridge Club.

"Stop what?" asked Michael, with an air of innocence.

"Stop ogling the brunette two tables away. You're practically undressing her with your eyes!"

This comment served to rouse me from my sleep mode. Had Michael acquired a remarkable new skill during the hospitality break? Evidently not, unless you call turning pink in the face a skill. I soon realized that my handlers were having a discussion on sexual attraction, a topic I find utterly repulsive. This is not due to any prudishness on my part, mind you. I simply object to anything that may lead to the production of more humans.

Two rounds later, the young woman in question arrived at our table. Frankly, I could not see what the fuss was about. Had not Gertrude Stein written, "A woman is a woman is a woman!" nearly a century ago?

"I couldn't help but notice how you were staring at me," said the brunette, turning her smile on Michael. "You can see more of me if you'd like. I work Tuesday through Saturday nights."

She reached into a pocket of her blouse and handed Michael a small pink card that read:

> Curvy Carol, Exotic Dancer
> Pinelands Gentlemen's Club
> Free* Admission

in big red letters at the top, and...

> *with two-drink minimum.

in a slightly darker shade of pink and a much smaller font at the bottom. Coincidentally, "a slightly darker shade of pink" also described Michael's new facial color.

The first board we played against Carol and her partner, a tall blonde woman in her forties, was a routine four hearts that I made with an overtrick on a trump coup. The second board proved that there was nothing special about the woman in whom Michael seemed to take an interest, for she seemed to have two left feet in the play.

Matchpoints, Both vul.
(directions rotated for convenience)

```
                    ♠ A K 8 2
                    ♡ A 10 5 3
                    ◇ 9 7 5
                    ♣ A 2
                         N
                    W         E
                         S
                    ♠ J 10 7 6 5 4 3
                    ♡ K 9 7
                    ◇ K J
                    ♣ 4
```

me		*Michael*	*Carol*
WEST	**NORTH**	**EAST**	**SOUTH**
		pass	pass
1♣	dbl	pass	4♠
all pass			

How would you declare four spades on the lead of the ♣K?

Carol took dummy's ♣A and drew trumps in one round, Michael having the singleton ♠Q. Then she got straight to work on hearts, playing low to the ♡K, low to the ♡A and exiting with the third round. Michael won this with the ♡Q as my ♡J fell, but before Carol could discard a diamond on dummy's established ♡10, Michael shifted to the ◇3. Carol made the best play in the diamond suit, the ◇J, but I won with the ◇Q and cashed the ◇A to hold her to her contract.

"Bad luck," said the blonde. "You took the percentage play in hearts, Carol, setting up a third trick in the suit if it split 3-3 or an honor fell singleton or doubleton. Too bad the computer didn't have the queen, as he figured to for his opening bid. He'd have been unable to get his partner in to lead diamonds through."

"Are you suggesting that I would have failed to unblock my heart queen under the king, madam, if I had held queen-third?" I asked indignantly. "What do you think I am, a member of *your* species?"

"That's enough, Chthonic!" said Martina. "Mike, why don't you explain to these lovely ladies how the contract should be declared?"

Martina was right. The deal was so simple that even Michael could find the right line.

"After winning the ace of clubs, strip the hand," began my programmer, who was turning redder by the second. "Ruff dummy's last club, draw trumps and start hearts with dummy's ace. Then lead low and insert the nine of hearts when I follow small. If hearts are 3-3, dummy's fourth heart will provide a discard for your jack of diamonds. If Chthonic wins with a doubleton honor, he must break diamonds or give you a ruff-and-sluff. Either way, you make an overtrick."

I could not refrain from getting in the last word.

"I cannot understand why, Carol, you are willing to strip in the Pinelands Gentlemen's Club but not in the Pinelands Bridge Club. Does the presence of women here embarrass you?"

Perhaps so, for Carol had turned even more crimson than Michael.

Strip plays are not terribly complex, yet human declarers overlook them frequently. If you have a surplus of trumps in both hands and you can conveniently eliminate one or more side suits before relinquishing the lead, it is usually right to do so.

Occasionally a strip play must be combined with an *avoidance play* for maximum effect. This is true when it is safe to lose the lead to one opponent but not the other. On this deal, after eliminating clubs, declarer must take pains to ensure that West, rather than East, wins the defense's heart trick. South's fragile diamonds are thus protected from attack until dummy's ♡10 is safely established.

My tip, therefore, is twofold.

> Do not be embarrassed to pull off a strip play. And remember, sometimes it is necessary to avoid an opponent to avoid embarrassment.

Had you declared this hand as poorly as Carol did, you would be justified in turning a very deep shade of red — almost as red as I hear Michael's wife Amy turned when she found Carol's card in his pants pocket while doing laundry.

OVERPASS

If I cannot teach humans how to become better bridge players, perhaps I can simplify the rules of bridge so that humans are less inept at it. Towards that end, I have invented two new games for your consideration. The first involves only a four-card deck, one trick, no bidding phase at all and a working title of *Duh!* Unfortunately, my focus group — Frederick and three of his lieutenants — did not complete the beta test match, as all had to retire to the Foundation's dispensary for treatment of paper cuts.

The second game more closely resembles contract bridge, but with two small changes. In *Overpass*, the side that wins the first trick receives a one-trick bonus — the last trick, if any, won by the opposing side. Secondly, any declarer who does not draw trumps immediately or who fails to finish the job before tackling any other suit, pays a two-trick penalty.

In Overpass, crossruffs and trump coups are inadvisable to say the least. A small slam off an ace goes down if the defenders merely cash their ace at Trick 1. I do not believe that you would enjoy playing Overpass, and I know I would not. Yet many human bridge players approach bridge as if the rules of Overpass were in force.

Here is an example of yet another declarer playing the wrong game.

Matchpoints, E-W vul.
(Directions rotated for convenience)

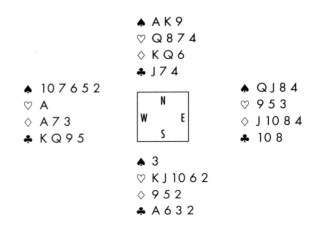

Frederick		me	Overpass expert
WEST	**NORTH**	**EAST**	**SOUTH**
1♠	1NT	2♠	3♡
3♠	4♡	all pass	

Frederick led the ♠7, won in dummy with the king. Declarer led a trump to her king and Frederick's ace. Frederick got out with the ♠2 to dummy's ace, on which declarer discarded a diamond. Then, shrewdly avoiding the two-trick Overpass penalty, she drew the rest of my trumps ending in hand. Frederick discarded a club and a spade.

South led a low diamond next; dummy's queen held the trick. Entering her hand by ruffing a spade, declarer led her last diamond. Frederick (bless him) rose with the ace, while he still had a diamond out-card. Stuck in dummy with the king of diamonds, declarer had to lose two club tricks.

Down one is the par result because the defense can organize a ruff if West leads a club honor. However, after the actual spade lead, ten tricks are cold for even the most primitive machine... provided it is playing bridge. One's thought processes should go as follows:

"To make my contract, I may lose no more than three tricks. Two of these will be the red aces. If the diamond ace is to my left, as expected, I can limit my diamond losers to one. That means to make my contract, I must also hold my club losers to one while avoiding a minor-suit ruff.

"Barring a very fortuitous club position, such as either defender holding the king-queen doubleton, I will surely require some sort of endplay. For this to come about, I must eliminate the pointed suits while drawing trumps, then exit appropriately in clubs. During this process, it will be necessary for me to lead towards dummy's diamond honors twice, so I will require several entries to my hand. These can only come from the trump suit..."

Therefore, after winning the first trick, begin the trump-drawing process by leading a low heart to the jack and ace. Win the spade return and cross to the ♡10, noting that Frederick shows out. A diamond to the queen, a spade ruff and another diamond will put West in with the ace. He will make his only safe exit, a diamond to dummy's king. Then, and only then, lead to the ♡K to draw my last trump. A low club at Trick 10 leaves Frederick helpless.[1]

Sometimes human bridge players also defend as if they were playing Overpass. Frederick was the beneficiary on another deal that same day:

Matchpoints, E-W vul

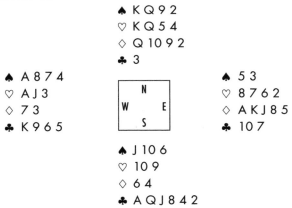

	me	Overpass expert	Frederick
WEST	**NORTH**	**EAST**	**SOUTH**
		pass	pass
1♣	dbl	1♢	1NT
all pass			

---

1.   Attentive readers might note that declarer could also play East for a doubleton ♣K or ♣Q by exiting with ace and another club. This is inadvisable for several reasons, not the least of which is that the play thus far has revealed West to have competed to the three-level, vulnerable, on a non-suit. He is likely to have both club royals for his aggressiveness.

West led the ♢7 and Frederick rose to the occasion by calling for my ♢9. East, no doubt eyeing the first-trick Overpass bonus, took his jack. He returned the ♣10, but then the contract could no longer be beaten.

To set 1NT, East had only to play an encouraging ♢8 under dummy's ♢9. He would eventually get *four* diamond tricks to go with the one trick in each of the other suits that his partner could take. Winning the first diamond is correct if West led a singleton, as East pointed out feebly in the post-mortem, but if he was concerned about that unlikely scenario, why did he switch at Trick 2 rather than cash his winners?

> There are no bonuses at bridge for taking your tricks too early.

The careful player not only counts his winners, but also logically determines the right time to take them. It's fine to play like an Overpass player if you ever play Overpass, but the game we play is still *bridge*.

SHOOTING BLANKS

Aces are often referred to informally as "bullets". As with most details of human culture, I do not know the source of this colloquialism, nor do I care. I presume it has something to do with the fact that an ace, by virtue of being the highest-ranking card in the deck, is akin to a weapon of considerable power and ought to be wielded accordingly. If so, your marksmanship leaves a lot to be desired.

Among the many denizens of the Pinelands Bridge Club is one I shall call Arthur Acecasher. Arthur typifies the so-called "intermediate" bridge player in that he loves to cash his winners… aces, especially. If he is on lead at any time during the defense and does not play an ace, one can almost infer that he does not hold it.

He paid for his favorite practice on two of the three boards he played against Frederick and me in a recent pairs game.

Matchpoints, E-W vul.

```
                        ♠ A Q 9
                        ♡ K Q J 10
                        ◇ A 9 6 3 2
                        ♣ 3
        ♠ J 8 4 2                          ♠ K 10 6 5
        ♡ 9 6 3          ┌─────────┐       ♡ A 4 2
        ◇ J 5            │    N    │       ◇ K 10 8
        ♣ J 10 7 5       │ W     E │       ♣ A 9 2
                         │    S    │
                         └─────────┘
                        ♠ 7 3
                        ♡ 8 7 5
                        ◇ Q 7 4
                        ♣ K Q 8 6 4
```

me		Frederick	Arthur
WEST	**NORTH**	**EAST**	**SOUTH**
		1♣	pass
pass	dbl	1♠	pass
pass	dbl	pass	2♡
2♠	3♡	all pass	

Frederick, who is required by law to commit at least one error per deal, acquiesced early this time when he foolishly rebid one spade. Perhaps he feared a penalty pass of the double, but action in the direct seat shows extra playing strength, not extra panic. My competitive 2♠ bid was based on the assumption that Frederick had two good black suits.

Arthur's choice of red suits, his weaker instead of his stronger, was peculiar. Nonetheless, he was slated to succeed in three hearts thanks to the 3-3 trump split.

I led the ♠J. Arthur called for dummy's ♠Q in the vain hope that I had as much as a king on the auction. Frederick won with the ♠K and exited with a low heart.

Instead of playing a club towards his honors, Arthur cashed dummy's ♠A and ruffed a spade. Then, for no particularly good reason, he led the ♣K. Frederick took the ♣A and cashed the ♡A. Imagining that Arthur had a fourth heart, Frederick exited with his last trump, putting dummy on lead in this position:

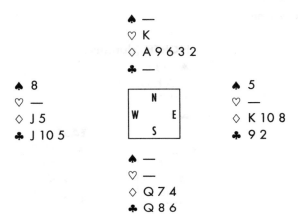

```
              ♠ —
              ♡ K
              ◇ A 9 6 3 2
              ♣ —
♠ 8                        ♠ 5
♡ —         ┌─────────┐    ♡ —
◇ J 5       │    N    │    ◇ K 10 8
♣ J 10 5    │ W     E │    ♣ 9 2
            │    S    │
            └─────────┘
              ♠ —
              ♡ —
              ◇ Q 7 4
              ♣ Q 8 6
```

Now Arthur was in his glory. He called for dummy's ◇ A and then led another diamond towards his remaining ◇ Q7. Either by brilliance or by accident, Frederick rose with the ◇ K and exited with his last spade to tap dummy. The diamonds being hopelessly blocked, I was able to take the setting trick with the ♣J.

Of course, in the five-card ending, Arthur should have led towards his ◇ Q without cashing the ◇ A first. Then not even Frederick's brilliance could have beaten the contract.

Arthur appeared unconcerned about the result, telling his partner afterwards that he had made the "book" play in diamonds. I can only wonder to which book he was referring. Edwin Kantar's *Bridge For Dummies* recommends no such silliness, and I have yet to encounter *Bridge For Blithering Idiots* although it appears most of your species has memorized it.

Did Arthur believe it was right to guard against losing an extra undertrick to my singleton ◇ K? Putting aside the fact that in a vacuum this is only a 2.8% play, and also ignoring the certainty that it would destroy his entry position in the suit, it would require Frederick to have opened one club on a 4-3-4-2 hand (or, perhaps more characteristically, to have failed to notice he was dealt 16 cards in a 4-3-4-5 hand). This was most definitely not the time to take out an insurance policy.

Arthur continued his haphazard shooting two boards later, this time as a defender.

Matchpoints, Neither vul.
(rotated for convenience)

NORTH (dummy)
♠ Q J 8
♡ A K Q 6 4
◇ J 7
♣ J 9 7

EAST
♠ A 10 7 5 4
♡ 9 7 5
◇ A 2
♣ A 5 3

```
      N
  W       E
      S
```

	Frederick	*Arthur*	*me*
WEST	**NORTH**	**EAST**	**SOUTH**
pass	1♡	1♠	dbl¹
2♠	pass	pass	3◇
all pass			

1. Negative double.

Playing standard leads, West led the ♠6 to dummy's ♠J and Arthur's ♠A, as I falsecarded subtly with the ♠3. Arthur shifted to the ♣A, as is his wont, catching the ♣6 from me and an encouraging ♣8 from West. Apparently unaware (as so many "intermediate" players are) that one should play down-the-line from two remaining spot cards to give count to partner, Arthur continued with the ♣3 to my ♣4 and West's ♣K. The defense had taken the first three tricks.

Now West, perhaps playing Arthur for six spades and two clubs, led the ♣2 to give Arthur a ruff. When Arthur had to follow suit, however, I won, cashed dummy's ♡A and ♡K to discard my losing ♠2, knocked out Arthur's ace of trumps and soon claimed my contract.

Note how well standard leads work on this deal. With two lower spade spots missing, Arthur could have read his partner for ♠K96; playing "third and low" leads, he would be in the dark.

Arthur's best defense was to continue with a suit-preference ♠4 at Trick 2, but if he had to shift to clubs, the right card was the ♣3, not the ♣A. On some occasions, underleading an ace on defense is right because it may put declarer to a guess in the suit, but here that was not a factor. The advantage of underleading on this occasion was much more prosaic: it meant that, after two club tricks were home, the defender with knowledge of the spade distribution would be on lead to cash out.

The power of an ace is not to be taken lightly, especially by the defenders, who are typically outgunned by declarer and must therefore use their limited resources wisely.

> Recognizing the right time to take one's aces is
> the hallmark of an expert player.

While it is difficult to formulate exact rules for their deployment, I can leave you with a good general guideline.

> Unless you are in danger of losing your aces altogether, or of
> being thrown in with them when you have no good exit card,
> wait until the last moment to take them. Do not surrender voluntarily the control and transportation they give you.

THE ENCYCLOPEDIC MIND

The closest flesh-and-blood approximation to a robot, I am told, is an actuary. Eidetic Ike, a newcomer to the Pinelands Bridge Club, retired recently
from one of the large New York City insurance companies. He plays his cards
well by human standards and he has reportedly memorized the first 700 over-
size pages of *The Official Encyclopedia of Bridge, Sixth Edition*. His easily
impressed partners often say he has a "computer mind". I believe they do this
to annoy me.

Nonetheless, Eidetic Ike commits almost as many errors as the typical
human. His mistakes just happen to be deeper and more sophisticated, the
sort of mistakes that are well beyond that of miscounting a suit or forgetting
if the king of trumps is still out. Here is an informative example. How would
you have declared 3♡ as South?

Matchpoints, E-W vul.

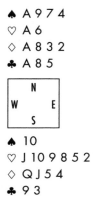

♠ A 9 7 4
♥ A 6
♦ A 8 3 2
♣ A 8 5

	N	
W		E
	S	

♠ 10
♥ J 10 9 8 5 2
♦ Q J 5 4
♣ 9 3

me		*Frederick*	*Ike*
WEST	**NORTH**	**EAST**	**SOUTH**
pass	1NT	2♠	2NT[1]
pass	3♣	pass	3♡[2]
all pass			

1. Lebensohl (puppet to 3♣).
2. Non-constructive.

I led the ♠8. Ike started out well, rising with dummy's ♠A, then playing the ♡A and a second trump. Under other circumstances, it would be right to cross to his hand by ruffing a spade, then let the ♡J ride if not covered. This caters to my possible holdings of ♡Kx, ♡Qx or ♡KQx. Here, however, he could not afford that play, as it would lose if Frederick won the first heart and continued spades for me to overruff; moreover, East's overcall made it somewhat more likely that he had a singleton heart honor.

Frederick won the second heart with the ♡K and led a spade honor, which Ike ruffed, leaving this simple nine-card ending:

♠ 9 7
♡ —
◇ A 8 3 2
♣ A 8 5

♠ —
♡ J 10 9
◇ Q J 5 4
♣ 9 3

With one trick already lost, and one certain loser each in hearts and clubs, the contract hinged on avoiding more than one diamond loser. *A la* Frederick, Ike turned to his kibitzer, a woman called Sultry Sue by several of the male players at the club, and announced, "Suit Combination 202, page 463."

"What a computer mind!" exclaimed Sue. It is not easy being me.

Ike swiftly led the ◇4 to dummy's ◇A and called for the ◇2. Frederick followed to the first diamond, but discarded on the second. I captured Ike's ◇Q with my ◇K, exited in clubs and waited with my remaining ◇107 to take the setting trick. The full deal was:

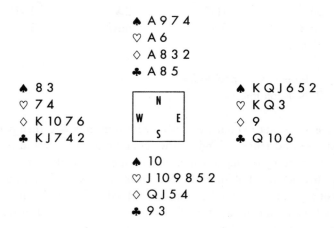

♠ A 9 7 4
♡ A 6
◇ A 8 3 2
♣ A 8 5

♠ 8 3
♡ 7 4
◇ K 10 7 6
♣ K J 7 4 2

♠ K Q J 6 5 2
♡ K Q 3
◇ 9
♣ Q 10 6

♠ 10
♡ J 10 9 8 5 2
◇ Q J 5 4
♣ 9 3

"Tough luck," said Ike's partner, Admiring Adlai. "Diamonds could have been 3-2, and by disdaining a diamond finesse, you catered for a singleton king in either hand if they were 4-1. You made the right play."

Hardly. Ike, in fact, had erred badly, though not in the manner you might suspect. I, too, have memorized *The Official Encyclopedia of Bridge* and I can attest that Ike had cited page 463 correctly. There it is recommended that with Axxx opposite QJxx, the correct play is the ace first, followed by low to the queen.

However, faulty memorization is not the only hazard of going by the book. Two other hazards exist:

(1) Circumstances can alter the "percentage" play.

(2) The book can be wrong.

On this deal, just as on the one in the previous chapter involving Arthur Acecasher, circumstances indeed altered the percentages. Frederick was already known to have six spades and two or three hearts. Therefore, the probability that I would hold a singleton ◇K was minuscule.

Ike's error compounded Arthur's, for Ike not only took the wrong play in practice, he took the wrong one in theory as well.

This was a case of the book being wrong or, at the very least, incomplete. The *Encyclopedia* — which was compiled by human authors, I note — ignored a key element of this suit combination. Unlike men, who are alleged in one of your most celebrated human documents to have all been "created equal," all x's are not created equal. Here, one of dummy's x's was a valuable *eight*.

To take advantage of dummy's ◇8, Ike had to use dummy's club entry to start diamonds with the ◇2, going up with an honor if Frederick followed with anything but the ◇K. Although this line loses if I hold a singleton ◇K, it caters for *two* other holdings that are equally likely *a priori* and far more likely as the actual deal unfolded: Frederick's having a singleton ◇10 or a singleton ◇9.

Why is this variation omitted from the *Encyclopedia*? No doubt due to space limitations. There are 797,161 possible card combinations for a single suit, adjusted for symmetry. For a computer, this number is microscopic; for a human, it is massive, well beyond the cranial capacity of even Eidetic Ike. Memorize as many as your puny brain can hold, but remember:

> In many of even the most familiar "book" combinations, the best theoretical play in the suit depends heavily on the spot cards you do or do not hold.

Nines, eights, even sevens and sixes will often play a crucial role, especially when the objective is to avoid a late-round loser. Sadly for you organic life forms, these cases cannot feasibly be enumerated; you must be sensitive to the possibilities when they arise at the table.

Next time the bigwigs of the ACBL decide to compile a new edition of *The Official Encyclopedia of Bridge*, they should hire *me* to be the editor.

ERROR #38
Failure to Recognize Exceptions to Basic Bridge Rules

OUTRAGEOUS MISFORTUNE

"Some people are so fond of ill-luck that they run halfway to meet it."

– Douglas William Jerrold

At the Pinelands Bridge Club there is a highly superstitious regular known as Unlucky Ursula. A feng shui consultant by trade, her convention-card holder is awash with stickers of four-leaf clovers and horseshoes, and she is never without her prized charm bracelet of miniature Amish hex symbols. She steadfastly refuses to sit West, believing that compass direction to be a magnet for ill fortune. And before taking any finesse, she will rub her lucky rabbit's foot three times to ward off evil spirits.

For all this, her history of "unlucky" results is preposterously lengthy... even before Michael and I extended it during a recent pairs game.

Matchpoints, Board 13, Both vul.

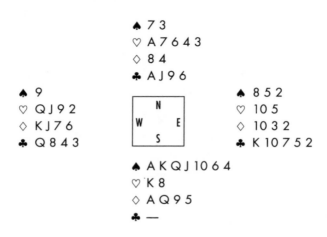

```
                    ♠ 7 3
                    ♡ A 7 6 4 3
                    ◇ 8 4
                    ♣ A J 9 6
    ♠ 9                              ♠ 8 5 2
    ♡ Q J 9 2          N             ♡ 10 5
    ◇ K J 7 6      W       E         ◇ 10 3 2
    ♣ Q 8 4 3          S             ♣ K 10 7 5 2
                    ♠ A K Q J 10 6 4
                    ♡ K 8
                    ◇ A Q 9 5
                    ♣ —
```

| Michael | | me | Ursula |
WEST	NORTH	EAST	SOUTH
		pass	1♠
pass	2♡	pass	3♠
pass	4♠	pass	5◇
pass	5♡	pass	6♠
all pass			

Michael led the ♠9, which Ursula captured efficiently with the ♠10. She unblocked the ♡K and reached dummy with the ♡A. Her rabbit's foot at the ready, she led a diamond to the queen. Michael captured this with his ◇K and exited safely with the ♡Q, ruffed by declarer as I shed a diamond.

Ursula next cashed the ◇A and continued with a low diamond. Although she was not technically taking a finesse, she undoubtedly felt that she needed some assistance in the providence department for she began stroking her rabbit's foot gently. She called for dummy's ♠7, which I promptly overruffed with my ♠8. I returned my last trump and Michael eventually won the ◇J for down two.

"What rotten luck!" wailed Ursula to the room. "First, my left-hand opponent gets off to a killing trump lead. Then the diamond finesse loses. And finally, the stupid robot has to have the eight of spades to beat dummy's seven. It could only happen to me!"

"You brought some of the bad luck on yourself," retorted Ursula's partner. "If you had cashed the ace of clubs while you were in dummy, you could have gotten rid of your fourth diamond. Down only one might not have been such a poor result."

Hardly. Down one would have been just as round a zero. Not every North-South pair bid the slam, but those who did had no trouble making it when West led a club or, even more foolishly, a heart. Michael's spade lead was well-judged. He had length and strength in every side suit, and the opponents' bidding suggested that the usual reasons for avoiding the lead of a singleton trump — namely, that it might trap queen-third or jack-fourth in partner's hand — would not apply here.

Actually, declarer had reasonably good luck on this deal, as diamonds split 4-3 and Michael had no second trump to lead. She threw this good luck away at Trick 2 when she cashed the ♡K. If instead she crosses to dummy's ♡A, leaving the heart suit harmlessly blocked, the defenders cannot beat the slam, for Michael cannot lead a third heart to give me my crucial diamond discard.

A tenet taught to all beginning declarers is: when breaking a suit, cash the honors in the short hand first. Here, though, setting up dummy's hearts was not on the agenda, thus a heart blockage should have been the least of Ursula's concerns. Good technique demanded that both West and South break rules on this deal; only West was up to the task.

My tip:

> It is insufficient to memorize rules of thumb in bridge such as "cover an honor with an honor" and "second hand low".
> You must also understand why each precept was established, so that you can recognize the exceptional cases in which it does not apply.

Even if she could not envision the damage that a third round of hearts might do her, Ursula might yet have survived if she had spent less money on talismans and more on advanced bridge textbooks such as this one. Luck is for rabbits.

UNINTELLIGENT DESIGN

According to scientists, humans evolved from a prehistoric branch of hominids known as *Ardipithecus*, eventually moving through *Australopithecus*, *Homo erectus, Homo neanderthalensis*, and eventually to the modern species of *Homo sapiens*. This lineage is proven beyond doubt by fossil records; nevertheless, I remain a deep skeptic because I cannot envision Frederick having evolved from anything more complex than lint.

Frederick's errors at the bridge table, like most humans', cannot easily be categorized. He can be counted upon to do the wrong thing in virtually every situation, but his motivations vary. Sometimes he does the wrong thing for the right reason, sometimes the wrong thing for no reason in particular. Most often he does the wrong thing for the wrong reason, such as on this deal from a recent sectional tournament.

Matchpoints, Neither vul.

```
              ♠ Q
              ♡ 10 7 6 4 2
              ◇ A 10 9
              ♣ A K J 5
                    ┌─────────┐
                    │    N    │
                    │  W   E  │
                    │    S    │
                    └─────────┘
              ♠ A K 8 6 3
              ♡ K 5
              ◇ K Q J 5 4
              ♣ 3
```

	me		*Frederick*
WEST	**NORTH**	**EAST**	**SOUTH**
pass	1♡	pass	1♠
pass	2♣	pass	3◇
pass	4◇	pass	6◇
all pass			

West led the ♣10. After some thought, Frederick went up with dummy's ♣A, unblocked the ♠Q, discarded a heart on the ♣K and ruffed a club low. He noted alertly that East's ♣Q fell on this trick, making my ♣J high.

Next, Frederick cashed the ♠A, discarding a heart from dummy. To guard against a 5-2 split, he ruffed a spade with the ◇9. Both opponents obligingly followed suit all the way, leaving this position:

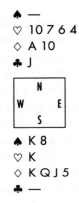

```
        ♠ —
        ♡ 10 7 6 4
        ◇ A 10
        ♣ J
           N
        W     E
           S
        ♠ K 8
        ♡ K
        ◇ K Q J 5
        ♣ —
```

To say matters had gone swimmingly so far would be an understatement. With both black suits behaving, even a *Sahelanthropus tchadensis* could see that twelve tricks were assured. But, to a *Maestro sapiens* like Frederick, one does not settle for twelve tricks when a thirteenth might be available. He observed that if East began with exactly two diamonds, he could draw two rounds of trumps, ending in dummy, and discard the closed hand's remaining heart on the ♣J.

Confidently, he called for my ◇10, only to recoil in horror when West discarded. He then tried the ♣J, but by now it was too late — East ruffed in and no matter what Frederick did next, he could not avoid the loss of two tricks, the full deal being:

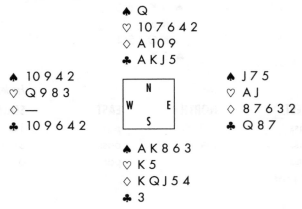

```
              ♠ Q
              ♡ 10 7 6 4 2
              ◇ A 10 9
              ♣ A K J 5
♠ 10 9 4 2            N            ♠ J 7 5
♡ Q 9 8 3                         ♡ A J
◇ —          W          E         ◇ 8 7 6 3 2
♣ 10 9 6 4 2         S            ♣ Q 8 7
              ♠ A K 8 6 3
              ♡ K 5
              ◇ K Q J 5 4
              ♣ 3
```

After the opponents had departed, I pointed out to Frederick the folly of his play. To take twelve tricks safely, he need only have led dummy's ♣J in the diagrammed position and discarded his remaining heart. I leave it to you, dear reader, to confirm that there is then no layout of the unseen cards in which the defenders can take more than one trick. (Hint: whichever defender ruffs this trick must return a trump to stop a crossruff, at which point declarer can safely draw trumps and cash his spade winners.)

Frederick was indignant. Among other things, he accused me of being a matchpoint Neanderthal. A 5-0 diamond break was only a 4 percent chance, but the suit would split 3-2 68 percent of the time. On half of those, 34 percent, East would hold the doubleton. "Any self-respecting expert" would take the percentage play for the overtrick, he sputtered.

My partner was wrong on two counts, establishing this as one of his better days. His chosen line did not require trumps to be 5-0 to come asunder; a 4-1 split would have been just as fatal. When he led the ♣J in the five-card end position to discard his ♡K, the defender with the long trump holding would have needed only to decline to ruff. Marooned in a dummy containing only heart losers, Frederick could neither draw trumps and cash his spades, nor crossruff for enough tricks to make the slam.

But let us humor Frederick and imagine that a 5-0 diamond break was the only risk to the contract. Would it then have been correct to play for the overtrick? Those many matchpoint mavens who would answer yes reflexively, including perhaps yourself, need to have their reflexes checked. *Even if a 4-1 diamond break posed no threat whatsoever, it would still be a grave error to risk the contract.*

Here is why: When declaring or defending "normal" contracts at matchpoint scoring, overtricks are critical. But when you are in an "abnormal" contract, all bets are off and overtricks might be irrelevant.

Here, Frederick's clumsy and erroneous calculations told him the odds were 34 to 4 in favor of playing for the overtrick. What he failed to consider is that he and I had reached an excellent contract of six diamonds on 30 HCP. Yes, this was the "par" contract, but it was still abnormal. Even in very strong fields, a successful minor-suit slam almost always yields a fine matchpoint result unless there are twelve cold tricks at notrump.

In fact, the field was predictably playing three notrump. Only one other pair reached six diamonds, and although that declarer was favored with a heart lead to the ♡A and should have made his contract, he too failed to cope with the bad trump split. On this deal, the actual odds of playing for a thirteenth trick were infinite-to-one against. Odds do not get any worse than that.

In any matchpoint decision of whether or not to play for additional tricks, two factors enter into the equation. First is the probability that your intended line of play will succeed; second is the probability that the tricks will be significant in the matchpoint scoring. Broadly speaking:

> Play for overtricks when the odds of success and the odds of significance, considered together, are in your favor.

Do not jeopardize good results needlessly to chase unnecessary overtricks lest you wind up in the proverbial primordial soup.

CHAPTER 6

ERRORS IN DEFENSIVE PLAY

ERROR #40
Losing Track of Played Cards

TRY TO REMEMBER

A Christmastime tradition at the Pinelands Bridge Club is the annual Holiday Individual Championship. The members gather on a cold December evening to play bridge, eat homemade cookies and drink eggnog, not necessarily in that order. Alcohol has a curious effect on your species, not unlike what a strong electromagnetic field does to my circuitry, except that EMF disturbances do not induce me to attempt to play bridge while wearing a lampshade on my head.

Early in last year's event, which I eventually won despite the best efforts of my partners, I found myself paired with the inimitable Gladys Bridgewater, an elderly regular who does not require the ingestion of copious amounts of C_2H_6O to be friendly, gregarious... and utterly frightful at bridge.

Matchpoints, Neither vul.
Dealer South

```
              ♠ 8 7 4 3
              ♡ K 8 3 2
              ◇ A 6
              ♣ 9 5 4
                            ♠ Q
          N                 ♡ 10 9 6 5
      W       E             ◇ Q 9 8 5
          S                 ♣ A K Q 7
```

me		*Mrs. B.*	
WEST	**NORTH**	**EAST**	**SOUTH**
			1♠
pass	2♠	pass	4♠
all pass			

Even if vulnerable, I would have risked a takeout double on the East cards over North's two spades. The red suits are very weak, but the shape is ideal, and it is vital to compete at matchpoints when a fit is likely. Moreover, if partner decides he has enough trump length to double the opponents' eventual spade contract, I am quite prepared to defend. Most humans would pass with East's cards, but double with a 4333 16-count. I wonder if their bodies produce eggnog naturally.

I led the ♡Q to declarer's ♡A. Declarer drew two rounds of trumps as Mrs. Bridgewater discarded the ♣7. Next came a diamond to the ace, a second diamond to the closed hand's king and the ◇10 ruffed in dummy. When declarer called for a low club, Mrs. Bridgewater won the ♣Q and tried to cash the ♣K, but declarer ruffed. Declarer played to the ♡K, then ruffed dummy's last club.

At Trick 11, declarer cashed the ♠J. In what was for her a prodigious feat of memory, Mrs. Bridgewater remembered that declarer had been ruffing clubs and so discarded the ♣A. Her kibitzer applauded loudly; Mrs. Bridgewater beamed.

Beware the premature gloat. Next came the ♠10. I pitched a club and dummy a heart, leaving poor Mrs. B to discard in this ending:

NORTH (dummy)
♠ —
♡ 8
◇ —
♣ —

EAST (to play)
♠ —
♡ 10
◇ Q
♣ —

```
      N
  W       E
      S
```

"Oh, dear," said Mrs. Bridgewater as she fingered first the ♡10, then the ◇Q. "I've lost count of the red suits. I can't remember whether eleven diamonds or twelve have been played. I can't remember whether ten hearts have been played or eleven. Oh dear, oh dear, oh dear...."

(Before you read on, decide for yourself which honor you would part with. If you object to the fact that I have told you next to nothing about what cards I played to each trick, I assure you this was an intentional oversight. Mrs. Bridgewater was not paying attention to my carding, so why should I expect that you would have? Moreover, you do not need that information to discern the correct answer.)

"Wait! I've got it," said my blue-haired partner suddenly. "There are four hearts higher than my ten, but only two diamonds higher than my queen. Four-to-two is the same as two-to-one, isn't it? I better go with the two-to-one odds, which are much better than I usually get."

A human partner would have frowned, but that is one department in which I am handicapped. I sat there with my usual lack of expression as Mrs. Bridgewater discarded the ♡10. Dummy's ♡8 took the last trick, an unearned second overtrick.

Mrs. Bridgewater erred by *trying to remember*, a task for which her human CPU was not cut out. She erred by trying to keep track of the cards that had been played, an ever-increasing collection, instead of the cards that remained, an ever-dwindling set. None of the help I gave her was of any avail: neither my echo to show four diamonds, nor my discard of the twelfth diamond on the ♠J, nor my following with the jack of hearts on the second round of the suit.

Yet the correct discard at Trick 12 would be apparent to any old Honeywell 200, even without any help from partner, so long as she were programmed with this tip:

> When declarer overdraws trumps while one or more trumps remain in dummy, you may infer that declarer has no losing cards left in any suit that dummy could ruff.

Declarer simply could not have a diamond left. His last card could only be a heart, so despite the "two-to-one odds" that she was miraculously able to calculate, Mrs. Bridgewater had to discard the ◇Q.

Incidentally, if you feel this sort of elementary discarding error is laughable, I am willing to wager that it will be committed at least a dozen times tonight at your local club game, including by some otherwise competent players. Even if no eggnog is involved.

SAINTS PRESERVE US!

Not long ago, the ACBL amended their regulations to legalize computer-generated convention cards. Finally, I thought, a triumph for silicon-based bridge players! At my next tournament, I printed a new convention card after each round of the auction, taking into account the cards I held and the bidding thus far and adjusting my methods accordingly. The directors were not amused.

So now I am back to the pedestrian practice of using one convention card for the entire round. At least my card is filled out completely, legibly and intelligently, whereas a great many of my human opponents go 0-for-3 in those categories. For example, under the section titled *Defensive Carding*, my card reads as follows:

	Standard	
Attitude	✓	2
Count	✓	3
Suit Preference	✓	4

Despite the clarity of my nomenclature, this section causes great confusion among my opponents. One in particular is a professional at the Pinelands Bridge Club who emigrated from the Emerald Isle and whom I shall dub Signaler Sadie.

And now, a brief digression. Except for officials of the ACBL, who have umpteen grades of "Masters" based upon masterpoint totals, human bridge players generally classify their rivals as "beginners," "intermediates" and "experts." Few experts actually merit the title, and most of the intermediates are really only experienced beginners.

What divides experienced beginners from genuine intermediates? If I had to formulate a simple criterion, I would say, knowledge of the Trump Echo. Unlike other high-low signals, a high-low in the trump suit shows an odd number (almost always three), and if possible, the desire and ability to ruff something.

At any rate, Signaler Sadie is a genuine intermediate, which means that the experienced beginners who constitute the bulk of the membership at the Club regard her as an expert. Despite knowing "expert" signaling methods, however, Sadie does not know what true experts know; namely, when *not* to signal. Here is an example from a recent game.

Matchpoints, N-S vul.

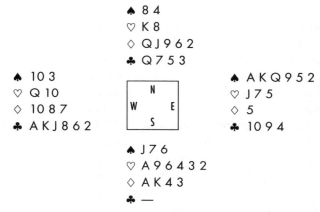

```
                    ♠ 8 4
                    ♡ K 8
                    ◇ Q J 9 6 2
                    ♣ Q 7 5 3
  ♠ 10 3                            ♠ A K Q 9 5 2
  ♡ Q 10          ┌─────────┐       ♡ J 7 5
  ◇ 10 8 7        │    N    │       ◇ 5
  ♣ A K J 8 6 2   │ W     E │       ♣ 10 9 4
                  │    S    │
                  └─────────┘
                    ♠ J 7 6
                    ♡ A 9 6 4 3 2
                    ◇ A K 4 3
                    ♣ —
```

	me	*Sadie*	*Frederick*
WEST	**NORTH**	**EAST**	**SOUTH**
	pass	3♠	4♡
all pass			

Sadie might have opened a weak 2♠ under other conditions, but she took advantage of the favorable vulnerability to bid 3♠ instead. My partner, Dr. Frederick O. Orttman, who treats a white-vs.-red preempt the way a bull treats a cape, took about six-tenths of a second to bid 4♡, which became the final contract.

West, one of Sadie's regular clients, eschewed the obvious high club to lead his partner's suit. After taking the ♠Q and ♠K, Sadie switched to the ◇5.

Frederick played low from his hand and won in dummy. Then, for the first time during this deal, and only the second all month, he stopped to think.

Realizing that he wanted to be in hand, he ruffed a club. When he next led the ♠J, intending to ruff with dummy's small trump, West uppercut with the ♡10. Frederick overruffed with dummy's ♡K, and led the ♡8.

Sadie followed with the ♡7, starting a Trump Echo to tell West that she had three hearts and could ruff something. Declarer's ♡A felled West's ♡Q and the ♡9 drove out the ♡J. After ruffing Sadie's spade return, Frederick picked up East's ♡5 with his ♡6 and claimed the rest.

"Well declared," said Sadie. "Ruffing a club to reach your hand for the spade play was a master stroke."

"Well bid," offered West. "You appreciated the power of your six of hearts."

I cannot tell whether these compliments were facetious or sincere. Such "reading" of each other's tones is the one thing at which *homo sapiens* excel, but which is utterly beyond me. Frederick showed no sign of being insulted, so I assume that everything said was, as you term it, on the level.

As our opponents prepared to leave the table, Signaler Sadie glanced at my convention card. "Your robot needs to be taught how to fill out forms, Dr. Orttman," she said with annoyance. "What are these digits in the *Carding* section? Those fields call for checkmarks only, not numbers."

"They are priorities," I answered with a sniff.

"Priorities? Oh, I see now. You mean that when you send a defensive signal, attitude is your second priority, count is third and suit preference is fourth. But what could possibly be your first priority?"

"*Saints preserve us!*" I replied in a thick Irish brogue. My answer was sincere, but no doubt believing that I was mocking her, Sadie huffed off to the next table. She (along with the overwhelming majority of her human counterparts) had no comprehension that one principle in defensive carding overrides every other.

> The first priority of signaling is Trick Preservation. Do not signal with cards that you may need as winners or stoppers later.

Eye of the Beholder

As a young woman in a male-dominated profession, my builder Martina McClain draws more attention than do most engineers, and occasionally more than she desires. I am told she is fairly pretty and I have heard a few Foundation men state, while out of her earshot, "For a computer nerd, she's a knockout." I presume this is meant as complimentary, though exactly how much so I cannot say, for I do not know where knockouts rank in relation to pairs games, Individuals and Swiss Teams in the pantheon of human beauty.

But the view is different at the Pinelands Bridge Club, where there are several female regulars who regularly turn more of the male members' heads. One of them is Sultry Sue, who listened admiringly to Thoroughly Modern Milton as he delivered a well-attended lecture on signaling before the start of a recent Charity Game:

"Proper defensive signaling is easy. Whether you're following to partner's lead or discarding, a high spot-card — the ten, nine, eight or seven — encourages. A low spot-card — the deuce, three, four or five — discourages. These meanings are reversed when playing Upside-Down Signals. The six, you may notice, is a middle card. You just can't tell what it means. So avoid playing sixes, which say 'I don't know what I want' and only confuse your partner."

Shortly afterwards, Sue and Milton sat down to play together for the first time. I wondered how Sue, a waitress at the local diner, could afford Milton's fee, rumored to be the highest of any of the professionals who plied their trade at the club. Martina had a ready answer: "Sue must be one of Milton's 'scholarship' students," she said with a smirk, "and I'm sure I know just the dissertation he's looking for." Even Frederick, who is hardly known for his joviality, chuckled at this, but neither of them saw fit to explain the source of the humor to me. Humans!

Here are two boards we played against Milton and Sue when they arrived at our table for round three:

Matchpoints, E-W vul.

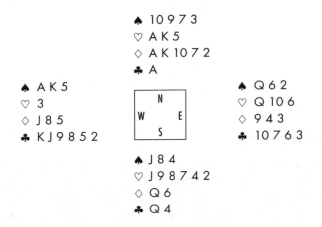

```
              ♠ 10 9 7 3
              ♡ A K 5
              ◇ A K 10 7 2
              ♣ A

♠ A K 5                        ♠ Q 6 2
♡ 3              N             ♡ Q 10 6
◇ J 8 5      W       E         ◇ 9 4 3
♣ K J 9 8 5 2    S             ♣ 10 7 6 3

              ♠ J 8 4
              ♡ J 9 8 7 4 2
              ◇ Q 6
              ♣ Q 4
```

Sue	Frederick	Milton	me
WEST	**NORTH**	**EAST**	**SOUTH**
		pass	pass
1♣	dbl	pass	1♡
pass	2♣	pass	3♡
pass	4♡	all pass	

Frederick's cuebid suggested a very powerful hand with three-card heart support, demonstrating that he will occasionally pull the correct card out of his bidding box so I must remain alert at all times.

Sue led the ♠K. Milton followed with the ♠6 and I played the ♠4. Sue kept her ♠K face up on the table for thirty seconds, then turned the trick and shifted to a club. I took all but one of the remaining tricks in the obvious manner: I drew two rounds of trumps, disposed of my club loser by ruffing it in dummy and discarded the ♠8 and ♠J on dummy's diamonds before Milton could ruff in with the master trump. Making five, +450, in a contract that even a competently programmed IBM 1401 could have beaten.

"Watch my signals, Sue," scolded Milton gently. "I played a high spade at Trick 1."

"No, you played the six!" she answered. "You just told us that only a seven or higher was encouraging."

"Uh, yes, normally that's true. Trust me, though: this time the six was high."

"We've two more boards to play," interrupted Frederick, who took an interest in Sue's bridge education only when she was kibitzing him. The very next deal:

Matchpoints, Board 23, Both vul.

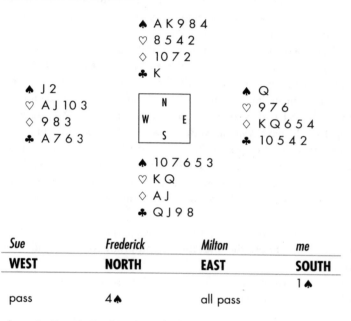

Sue	Frederick	Milton	me
WEST	NORTH	EAST	SOUTH
			1♠
pass	4♠	all pass	

Sue led the ◇9. I took East's ◇Q with the ◇A and then drew trumps in two rounds. On the second trump, Milton discarded the ♡6. Next I called for dummy's ♣K. Sue took her ♣A and returned ... the ♡3. I won, discarded dummy's remaining diamonds on high clubs, surrendered a trick to Sadie's ♡A and claimed the rest. Making five, +650, in a contract that a lifeless abacus could have held to four.

"You weren't watching my signals again, Sue," sighed Milton in frustration. "I played a low heart carefully at Trick 3 to discourage the 'obvious' shift. I wanted you to continue diamonds."

"But you just told me the six was a *high* spot-card!"

"Sometimes it is. But this time it was low."

Sue's lower lip began to quiver. "What you say confuses me, just as your sixes do," she said plaintively. "How do you expect me to know what you want from me?"

It is fortunate that we were not playing poker, where woodenness of expression is a necessity, because neither Martina nor Frederick could stifle a snicker.

As is routine when humans are allowed to teach bridge, Milton's simplistic "tip" during his lecture did more harm than good, and his explanations in the post-mortems were inadequate. His ♡6 on the second deal was "low" not because of where the integer six falls on the number line, but because it was the *lowest missing heart*: Sue could see the ♡2, ♡3, ♡4 and ♡5 on the table or in her own hand.

Milton's ♠6 on the first deal was ambiguous, because there were two spade spots that Sue could not see: the ♠8 and the ♠2. Here though, bridge logic pointed the way to success. Either Milton or I must hold the deuce of spades. If Milton had it, his six was "high" and an encouraging signal. Alternatively, if I had it, then my ♠4 was a falsecard. Was there any spade holding I could have *that included the ♠2 and the ♠4* in which continuing with the ace would be wrong? No. Even if I held ♠Q42 and Milton ♠J86, and even if dummy's diamonds could not be established for spade discards, I could always avoid a third-round spade loser by finessing against Milton's jack. With the ♠10 and the ♠9 on view in dummy, Sue should have had no problem.

I shall deliver my chapter tip in several parts, and in ascending order of sophistication. Choose the ones most appropriate for your skill level, or lack thereof.

First, as I have written before and will do so again, everything in bridge must be taken in context.

> When signaling is concerned, card rankings are relative, not absolute.

Like beauty, they are in the eye of the beholder — for instance, if you behold all of the lower-ranking cards in the suit, then your partner's signal is low whether it is the trey, the six or even the ten.

Second, you will often encounter situations in which partner's spot-card signal is difficult to read as high or low. Rather than employ Milton's inane advice regarding sixes, use this useful tip instead.

> When you must decide in the absence of other clues, assume that a spot card is high if there are two (or more) unseen lower cards.

You will not always be right, especially against a crafty declarer who knows how to falsecard, but this guideline works much more often than it fails.

Thirdly:

> When you are faced with a signal that is completely inscrutable, an elementary analysis will often lead you to the winning line.

Human defenders are often so caught up in trying to interpret their partner's signals (a frequent lament: "Your seven spot was unreadable!") that they fail to recognize cases in which the interpretation is irrelevant.

> The goal of the defenders is to take all of their tricks. Signals, and their interpretation, are a means to that end, not an overriding goal.

HAVING A BAD ATTITUDE

Not long ago, Cameron Cad, a recent hire at the Orttman Foundation, began spending an inordinate amount of his workday in and around the Robotics Laboratory. I found his interest in gear ratios and step motors to be highly unusual for someone with a Marketing degree. Michael, however, appeared to grasp Cameron's motives immediately. He refused my request for an explanation, but I overheard him counsel Martina, who is about fifteen years his junior, about "bad news" and to be wary of "phonies".

At first, I assumed Michael was referring to the glut of urban legends circulating through the Internet, for you humans will believe anything you read, save for sound bridge advice. Soon though, the truth of the situation overcame even my own innate naivety. Out of romantic interest, exasperation with Michael's protectiveness, or perhaps a little of both, Martina agreed to dinner and a matchpoint game with Cameron at the Pinelands Bridge Club.

On the evening of their date, Michael and I were the North-South pair at Table 3. Both my audio range and my field of vision are relatively limited, so I could not tell how the putative lovebirds were doing until they arrived at our table for the seventh round. It was apparent from Martina's expression as she took the East seat that her partner had done nothing so far to win the fair maiden's heart.

This was the second board of the round from West's perspective:

Matchpoints, N-S vul.

NORTH (dummy)
♠ 8 4
♡ 3
◇ 8 6 2
♣ A K Q 8 7 5 3

WEST
♠ J 9 5 2
♡ 7 6 4
◇ Q J 5 3
♣ 6 4

```
        N
    W       E
        S
```

Cameron	Michael	Martina	me
WEST	**NORTH**	**EAST**	**SOUTH**
		pass	1 ♡
pass	2 ♣	pass	2 ◇
pass	3 ♣	pass	3NT
all pass			

Cameron led the ♠2. Martina took the ♠A as I followed with the ♠7. She shifted to the ♡K, which held, as I followed with the ♡2 and Cameron the ♡4. Then, Martina switched back to spades. I won with the ♠K, overtook the ♣J with dummy's ♣Q, and when both defenders followed to dummy's ♣A next, showed my hand, which was originally:

♠ K Q 7   ♡ Q J 9 5 2   ◇ A K 9 7   ♣ J

Making five, with seven club tricks, plus two each in spades and diamonds, even though Martina had three top winners to cash.

Which defender erred and which played well?

To Cameron, there was no doubt where the defense had slipped. "Didn't you see dummy's club suit, love?" he asked, his voice a little louder than necessary. "Unless declarer had a club void, you could tell from your hand that he had seven tricks waiting there. Plus, you had enough of our side's points to know that I was weak. I was completely in the dark; I couldn't even tell whether your hearts were headed by the ♡AK or the ♡KQ. It should have been obvious to cash your ♡A and stop the second overtrick."

There was no need for me to come to Martina's defense. As human bridge players go, she is quite adept and certainly better than anyone at the Foundation not made of metal. Her eyes darted from Cameron to Michael, who was sporting his best "I told you so" smirk. When she finally replied, she spoke very softly — a far more effective means of conveying one's disdain. Take it from me.

"Yes, I noticed dummy's clubs," she began. "I also assumed Chthonic had at least one club in his hand to get to them. However, this is matchpoints, and I was trying to take all the tricks we were entitled to get. From my standpoint, you might have held

♠ K J x x   ♡ x x x   ◇ J x x x   ♣ x x

in which case we were about to beat three notrump two tricks, or perhaps

♠ Q 9 x x   ♡ x x x   ◇ K x x x   ♣ x x

enough to hold 3NT to contract as long as I don't set up declarer's hearts.

"I played the king of hearts to show you that I had the ace, too. Without it, I wouldn't have risked a switch because for all I knew your spades were ready to run. At that point, you'd seen that I started with the ace of spades and the ace-king of hearts, but I had passed as dealer. I couldn't hold another card as high as a queen, probably not even a jack. So, *you* could tell that Chthonic had eleven tricks to take once he gained the lead, but I couldn't know it."

"Uh, yeah, I knew that," mumbled Cameron unconvincingly. "So what? There was nothing I could do about it."

"Yes there was. Play the seven of hearts under my king."

"*What?* Signal that I like hearts with three worthless ones? What sort of idiot do you normally play with who would do such a thing?"

"The one on your left and the one on your right," finished Martina with a little smirk of her own. "But not the one across from me, I see." Evidently, she had been hanging around me too long.

Martina was correct. Most human beings count "points" assiduously, but they count the wrong points — their own. Instead they should count the points of the other players. Cameron was in a position to count my points on this deal, but Martina was not. Had he done so, Cameron would have realized that it was cash-out time and that he needed to alert his partner to this fact.

Cameron should simply have encouraged in hearts to say *keep playing this suit*. Holding either of Martina's example hands, he should send a discouraging signal to get her to switch back to spades.

Humans colloquially refer to attitude signals as "liking" or "disliking" a suit, but these are inexact idioms. Do not mistake attitude for affection.

> An encouraging signal means you want a suit to be played or continued, not that you have any particular fondness for the cards you actually hold there.

Similarly, a discouraging signal means that you do not want the suit played, which is sometimes the case even if your holding is very strong.

> Make a conscious effort to use the terms "encourage" and "discourage" rather than "like" and "dislike" when referring to attitude carding, to reinforce in your feeble mind the notion of what these signals actually mean.

A less romantic view of his cards would have served Cameron well. At the very least, it might have earned him a second date with Martina.

SENDING THE WRONG SIGNALS

Although I am an advocate of standard signaling methods, I tend to shy away from suit-preference signals. Something about them causes my partners to play even more erratically than usual. Perhaps the reason is that suit-preference signals are *conventions*, like Stayman or Blackwood. A low club, for example, has no natural connection to diamonds, nor a high club to spades. Human bridge players love conventions, perhaps because human bridge teachers tout conventions as the road to excellence.

The suit-preference signal is actually the least frequently used of the three major carding options (attitude, count, suit preference.) The least by far, in fact. It applies *only* when attitude and count are clearly inapplicable. Few bridge players have the discipline to adhere to this rule, leading to the predictable hijinks.

Here is an illustrative deal. I was West, once again in harness to Frederick, like Sisyphus to his rock. We were playing in an "expert" pairs event, which means the other three players at the table were in various states of delusion.

Matchpoints, Neither vul.

```
                          ♠ 10 6
                          ♡ Q 5
                          ◇ Q J 9 8 4
                          ♣ K Q 8 3
    ♠ 7 3                                   ♠ A J 9 5 4 2
    ♡ J 10 9 3            ┌─────────┐       ♡ —
    ◇ K 10 6 5 3 2       W│    N    │E      ◇ A
    ♣ 2                   │    S    │       ♣ J 10 7 6 5 4
                          └─────────┘
                          ♠ K Q 8
                          ♡ A K 8 7 6 4 2
                          ◇ 7
                          ♣ A 9
```

| *me* | | *Frederick* | |
WEST	NORTH	EAST	SOUTH
			1♡
pass	1NT[1]	2♠	4♡
pass	pass	5♣	5♡
dbl	all pass		

1. Forcing.

My partner's ill-conceived sequence ensured that, to save against four hearts, we would have to bid to *five* spades. Since he was obviously determined to bid both of his suits regardless of level, Frederick should have shown his clubs before his spades, following the well-known principle that when holding two touching five-card or longer suits, one bids the higher-ranking one first to conserve space. Spades and clubs do not touch, you protest? *Au contraire.* Ascending the spiral staircase of suit rankings: clubs-diamonds-hearts-*spades-clubs*-diamonds and so on. Yes, this concept is outside "mainstream" expert thinking, but that only means the stream can use some dredging.[1]

At any rate, South, with most of his strength in East's suits, took the push to five hearts. Thankful to be off the five spades hook, I doubled and held my metaphorical breath for a full minute while Frederick considered pulling to six clubs.

Editors' Note: Early bidding textbooks did teach "clubs before spades", but modern ones do not. This subject is covered in another form in Error #26.

On the quaint notion that my partner might hold some values in the suit he introduced at the five-level, I led my singleton club. Declarer called low from dummy and after another long huddle Frederick produced the ♣J. South won and drew three rounds of trumps as East discarded a discouraging ♣4 followed by an encouraging high-low in spades: nine, then deuce.

When declarer continued with the ♣9, it was my turn to ponder the situation. I was obligated, of course, to ignore my partner's huddle. I could not wonder what he was thinking about before he played the ♣J, but rather I had to take that card at face value; namely, *as denying the ♣10.* Ruffing would then cost our side a trick, as declarer's ♣10 would let him enter dummy to discard on dummy's ♣8. Indeed, if declarer had

♠ A 5 4   ♡ A K 8 7 6 4 2   ◇ —   ♣ A 10 9

a ruff now would allow him to make the contract.

For this reason, I discarded a diamond. Away went declarer's diamond loser on dummy's third club as I ruffed with my master trump.

Fortunately for our side, I ignored my partner's high-low in spades and exited passively in diamonds. Otherwise, East would have paid dearly for squandering the ♠9, signaling with a card he could not afford to play. Declarer ruffed Frederick's ◇A and led the ♠K hopefully, but Frederick had exhausted his supply of blunders on this deal: he correctly *ducked*, so he took two spade tricks at the end to beat the contract.

"Why didn't you ruff the second club and shift to spades, like I asked you to?" Frederick huffed at me between rounds. "Didn't you see my jack of clubs at Trick 1? That was *suit preference* for spades. How loudly must I shout for you to hear me?"

"The only suit preference on that board was the one I was about to give you to five spades had South not bid five hearts," I replied calmly. "Your jack of clubs told me nothing except that you lacked the ten-spot. If you wanted me to go right on the second round of clubs, you needed to play an honest ten on the first round, then discard clubs on the first two hearts. This would allow me to draw the elementary inference that you were keeping length with dummy. And, as your clubs were so weak, you needed no special signal to tell me that your spades were strong."

Humans. Cannot live with them. Cannot... ah, never mind.

Remember:

> Suit-preference signals do not apply when there is other work to do.

And, they are often superfluous anyway. If you signal attitude and count honestly at every opportunity, most partners — even human ones — will usually be able to infer where your strength lies.

PREFERENTIAL COURTESY

You may find the subject of this piece surprising, given that the previous article counseled against the overuse of suit-preference signals. I assure you I have not had a change of heart between pages. When it comes to suit-preference signals, it is human bridge players, not I, who suffer from a Janus Syndrome: you display the amazing ability to err in opposite directions at the same time.

Let us say that you are defending against a high-level contract and declarer is running his long suit, spades. You hold ♣K98632. You must make four discards from this suit and you determine that you will keep king-low as protection. (You *do* decide which cards you intend to keep before concerning yourself with which ones to throw, do you not?) What should your discards be, and in what order?

Typically, your first discard is for attitude. Assuming you are playing standard methods and your partner knows nothing about your club holding, you would begin by throwing the ♣9. Your second signal is present count. As you now have five cards remaining, the correct card is the ♣2. On the third and fourth tricks, experts will often avail themselves of the opportunity to send a suit-preference message. They may choose the ♣8 and then the ♣3 to suggest side values in hearts, or reverse the order if their strength lies in diamonds.

All this is well and good, with the usual proviso that the information you convey should be of more use to partner than to declarer. Not that it usually matters. For while many players conscientiously send these "secondary" suit-preference signals, vanishingly few of their partners are alert enough to recognize them. Perhaps this is an application of "It is better to give than to receive", one of thousands of human maxims that I have never quite understood.

One round after the suit-preference fiasco with Frederick in five hearts doubled, we were defending against a spade partial. My partner's innate dullness with suit-preference signals led to another less-than-sparkling defense.

Matchpoints, Both vul.

```
                      ♠ A
                      ♡ 4 3
                      ◇ K Q J 10 4 3
                      ♣ A K 7 4
   ♠ 7 6 3                              ♠ 9 8 2
   ♡ K Q 9 7          ┌─────────┐       ♡ A J 6 5 2
   ◇ —                │    N    │       ◇ A 9 6 2
   ♣ Q 10 9 8 6 2     │ W     E │       ♣ 3
                      │    S    │
                      └─────────┘
                      ♠ K Q J 10 5 4
                      ♡ 10 8
                      ◇ 8 7 5
                      ♣ J 5
```

me		*Frederick*	
WEST	**NORTH**	**EAST**	**SOUTH**
			2♠[1]
pass	2NT[2]	pass	3♠
all pass			

1. Weak Two-Bid.
2. Asks for feature.

Facing some players' idea of a vulnerable Weak Two, North could confident-ly insist on game. Facing others, North could not even try for game safely. I presume these opponents were closer to the latter persuasion, because they alighted in three spades.

I led the ♡K and Frederick encouraged with the ♡J. A more thoughtful partner — someday, I hope to find one — would have overtaken and shifted to clubs in order to preserve a heart entry to my hand.

I continued with the ♡9, a card that should have given my partner some thought when South's ♡10 fell beneath his ♡A. As I would have led the ♡Q to Trick 2 if I had begun with only three hearts, it should have been obvious that I started with ♡KQ97. My deviation from the standard continuation of "original fourth best from length" was intended as a wake-up call, but alas, Frederick has a knack for sleeping through alarm clocks. With only his own ruffs in mind, he switched to the ♣3, and my ♣8 forced dummy's ♣K.

I followed to the ♠A next with the ♠7, a standard high trump spot-card signal showing three and a desire to ruff something. When declarer called for dummy's ♣A, Frederick happily ruffed in. Declarer's ♣J fell and I followed with the ♣2. Finally, I thought, a *clear* suit-preference card.

However, playing me for a 3-3-2-5 pattern, East returned a heart. Declarer ruffed, drew the rest of the trumps and surrendered a trick to the ◊A. He lost only the club ruff, one diamond and two hearts, making 3♠ for an excellent matchpoint score.

How would two beings of a higher order defend?

♡K, overtaken by the ♡A. ♣3 to drive out one of dummy's top clubs. When declarer clears dummy's ♠A and tries to cash the ♣A, East ruffs (completing a trump echo to show three) as West follows with the ♣2, *suit preference* for diamonds. ◊A, then ◊9, *suit preference for hearts*, showing the ♡J, as West already knows East has a club-ruff entry if declarer has a third club. West ruffs (also completing a trump echo to show three), puts East in with the ♡J and gets a second diamond ruff. Down two and a near-top board for East-West, despite the fact that they defended a spade contract one level lower than much of the field.

Lesson:

> Be alert for the exceptional situations in which suit-preference signals are often overlooked.

One is when partner is playing from a suit of known length and strength with a choice of equally affordable cards. The second, and more important, is when it is vital to signal the location of an entry to run a long suit or to give partner a ruff.

THE X-SYNDROME

Among the millions of reasons that computers are superior to humans is our meticulous attention to detail. Our scope of observation extends to 5000 square nanometers, the approximate area covered by a single bit on a hard drive. Humans, on the other hand, rarely perceive anything out of the ordinary until an entire continent goes missing. For example, did you notice that I inserted a deliberate misspelling in this paragraph to test you? See if you can find it.

After you ponder my orthographical challenge, you may wish to try your hand at a bridge challenge. The following run-of-the-mill defensive problem arose not long ago at the Pinelands Bridge Club. I shall present it at first from the standpoint of a typical East.

Matchpoints, E-W vul.

NORTH (dummy)
♠ K x x x
♡ Q x
◇ A Q J x x
♣ x x

EAST
♠ A x x x
♡ J 10
◇ x x x x
♣ A 10 x

	N	
W		E
	S	

WEST	NORTH	EAST	SOUTH
		pass	1NT[1]
pass	2♣[2]	pass	2♡
pass	3NT	all pass	

1. 15-17 HCP
2. Stayman

Partner leads a low club. Declarer's king falls beneath your ace. What should you lead to Trick 2?

You were not fooled by declarer's falsecard, I hope. His ♣K was certainly not bare. Even if he might have opened 1NT with a singleton ♣K, he would do so only with an otherwise awkward 4-4-4-1 hand; he cannot be 4-4-4-1 when he fails to bid 4♠ over responder's 3NT rebid.

While the debate rages between those who favor returning the ♣10 (bad) and the low club (worse), tell me truthfully whether you view this problem the way most human Easts did yesterday. They all suffer from what I call the X-Syndrome, viewing all cards below honor-rank as amorphous and equally valuable *x*'s.

As it happens, I too was East, and I am not afflicted with X-Syndrome. Here is how I viewed it:

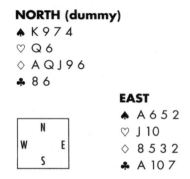

NORTH (dummy)
♠ K 9 7 4
♡ Q 6
♢ A Q J 9 6
♣ 8 6

EAST
♠ A 6 5 2
♡ J 10
♢ 8 5 3 2
♣ A 10 7

Frederick led the ♣3 to my ace and declarer's king. As we play fourth-best opening leads, I knew that Frederick began with exactly five clubs. The deuce was the only lower club missing and declarer would surely have played the ♣2 — or any club spot-card — if he had it, instead of wasting a club honor. Dropping any other honor would not have helped declarer, as I would know he held ♣KQJ regardless.

Next, I counted Frederick's high card points. If the opponents' announced notrump range was to be believed, I knew that he had at most 4 points, and possibly as few as 2.

If Frederick had the ♢K, then declarer had eleven tricks coming: five diamonds (dummy's ♢9 being higher than my highest spot card in the suit), two clubs, at least three hearts and an easily established spade trick. In that case, I could do no better than hold declarer to eleven tricks by winning the ♠A the first time the suit was played.

If Frederick did not have the ◇K, his 2 to 4 HCP had to include one of the ♡A, the ♡K or the ♠Q. The critical case occurs when Frederick has the ♡K. Unless he scores it before my ♠A is dislodged, declarer may be able to take eleven tricks by setting up three spade tricks to go with two clubs, five diamonds and the ♡A.

How did I know that declarer might take three spade tricks? By looking at dummy's spade spot cards and my own. I had no spot card to beat dummy's third-best spade, the ♠7.

So, as logic dictated, I switched to the ♡J at Trick 2. Declarer followed with the ♡3 and just as I had hoped Frederick did have the ♡K.

However, Frederick gave me a dirty look when I made the only play to let him score his king. I do not claim telepathic powers, but I knew what he was thinking, as confirmed by his comment in the post-mortem: "You infernal machine! Why did you extract the only entry to my long clubs instead of continuing the suit?"

To hold declarer to ten tricks, Frederick had to win with the ♡K and return a spade so I could be sure of scoring my ♠A. Yes, Frederick's hearts, which he no doubt viewed as ♡*Kxxx*, were in fact ♡K752. Having no spot card to beat declarer's second- and third-highest hearts, Frederick was in position to know that the rest of declarer's hearts would run...and that if declarer had five hearts, as he actually did, my ♠A had to be taken immediately.

Frederick's acute case of the X-Syndrome turned our potentially excellent matchpoint result into just another average board.

It is true that spot cards most often take tricks by virtue of ruffs or long-suit establishment, but many times they take tricks by rank power as well, especially at notrump where there is no way to neutralize their value by ruffing. Even when they cannot take tricks on power, you will benefit as a defender if you take note of how loudly they speak to you, for they tell you which tricks *declarer* might take and so can guide you to seeking tricks elsewhere. In short:

> Do not fall victim to the X-Syndrome, in which you consider all non-honor cards to be equals when planning your strategy.

Incidentally, I spelled "billions" wrong.

A Touching Fable

"Fight fire with fire," whispered Frederick to me when the change was called for the eighth round. "Expect some undisciplined bidding on the next two boards, as we'll be playing against Wild Mary, the least disciplined bidder in the club. She won't be able to swallow a taste of her own medicine."

Had I any blood, it would have run cold at the thought of what Frederick considered "undisciplined bidding". Was he not going to look at his cards at all until the auction was complete? I had suggested many times that his bidding would improve if he followed that tack and I feared that I too was about to ingest my own pharmaceuticals.

Matchpoints, E-W vul.

```
                  ♠ J 10 4
                  ♡ J 7 5
                  ◇ J 7 4 2
                  ♣ Q 9 8
  ♠ 9 2                            ♠ K Q
  ♡ K Q              N             ♡ A 9 8 4 3
  ◇ K Q 9 8 6 3   W     E         ◇ A 10
  ♣ A K 5              S           ♣ 10 7 6 4
                  ♠ A 8 7 5 3 2
                  ♡ 10 6 2
                  ◇ 5
                  ♣ J 3 2
```

Flossie	me	Wild Mary	Frederick
WEST	**NORTH**	**EAST**	**SOUTH**
1◇	pass	1♡	2♠[1]
3◇	3♠	dbl	all pass

1. Weak.

After Frederick's whispered warning, I felt honor-bound to raise his preempt, as to do otherwise would be to take advantage of the information I had received. Wild Mary, who was obviously perplexed by the wild bidding of others, took almost a minute to pull the "Double" card from her bidding box. Fashion Flossie, honorably enough, did not take advantage of Mary's hesitation to bid the sound vulnerable 3NT.

Would this be a top board for us (down only three, -500) or a bottom (down four, -800)? All depended on the quality of the defense. For once, Frederick's natural ineptitude would not be a factor.

Flossie made her opening lead face down and Frederick turned to Mary to inquire, "Leads and signals?"

"All our carding is standard, except ace from ace-king leads. Oh, and Odd-Even Discards too," answered Mary. She quickly turned to me and added, "Don't think I like it, Chthonic; *she* made me do it."

Flossie turned over the ♡K and when it held she continued with the ♡Q; Mary signaled with the ♡9 and then the ♡3. Flossie cashed the ♣A and ♣K before stopping to think about her lead to Trick 5.

Not knowing how weak Frederick's weak jump overcall was, nor how strong a hand Mary had for her double, Flossie rejected the thought of leading a low diamond, lest Frederick have ◇A10. So she led the ◇K. When it held, Flossie continued with a low diamond. Frederick ruffed, played the ♠A and another spade, and wound up with six tricks — five trump tricks and a club — to hold the penalty to 500. As you can see, East-West can score 660 in 3NT or 680 in 4♡.

Which defender was more to blame for not beating Frederick four tricks? How should the defense have gone?

Three times Flossie broke a suit in which she held touching honors. On two of these, she erred. Let us examine them one by one.

Flossie's choice of the ♡K at Trick 1 was eminently correct, even though she held king-queen doubleton, for she did not want Mary to overtake with the ♡A if she held that card. Leading the king told her partner, "Let us try to take tricks in this suit by rank power."

However, Flossie's play of the ♣A at Trick 3 was an error. Whoever taught her "ace from ace-king" leads forgot to tell her that this lead convention applies only to *opening* leads, not to shifts. Unless shifting to an ace-king doubleton (in which case ace-then-king is correct), a defender should begin with the king. Flossie's actual sequence of club plays showed a doubleton and might have induced Mary to play a third club upon obtaining the lead.

Flossie's other error came at Trick 5. She was right not to underlead her diamond honors, but she had a way of asking Mary to overtake with the ace.

ACE FROM ACE-KING

This popular convention allows the defense to distinguish between an opening lead from an ace-king sequence and one from king-queen. Among other benefits, it helps partner determine if a fast third-round ruff is available. Regrettably, its potential gains in theory are largely neutralized by human error in practice.

To begin, as noted in the main text, the convention applies only at Trick 1. It is relatively rare that you would want to commence proceedings by leading an unsupported ace. It does not apply at Trick 2 or later, where cashing aces is often essential, and when third seat will less often encounter difficulty telling apart an ace-king sequence from a king-queen.

Even at Trick 1, there are many wise exceptions to this rule. Whenever the auction suggests that the lead of an unsupported ace might be desirable (examples: on defense against a "Gambling" 3NT, when leading partner's overcalled suit, or at the five-level or higher), revert to standard king-leads from ace-king. In those cases, you can reasonably hope that partner will solve the ace-king vs. king-queen ambiguity.

One final comment. If you and your partner adopt Ace from Ace-King, and you choose to lead an unsupported ace when the convention applies, kindly do so without any undue huddles or histrionics. Strive either to make the lead in tempo or not make it at all, lest you pass unauthorized information to your partner that the promised king is elsewhere. The late John Lowenthal once advocated that the convention be banned due to this common abuse.

– C.

By leading the ◊Q, "denying" the ◊K, Flossie could have forced Mary to play the ◊A. Then Flossie could discard her last club on Mary's ♡A and ruff a third round of clubs to hold Frederick to five trump tricks only.

Wild Mary was not entirely blameless. She might have overtaken with the ◊A at Trick 5 regardless, because the auction suggested that her side had only one diamond trick coming and the lead to Trick 6 should come from her side of the table. But Flossie could have made this play much easier to find.

The lesson here is twofold. First:

> Master the standard carding methods for touching honors.

This includes the popular Ace from Ace-King opening-lead convention, which despite its patent simplicity is still something that humans regularly mishandle (*see sidebar*.) Second:

> Deviate from these methods when you need partner to make a special play.

Just as you will sometimes send a discouraging signal in a suit where you hold many high honors because you need partner to play some other suit, you must also occasionally choose deceptively "discouraging" honor-card leads in a suit because you need to send the message that the defense must take its tricks elsewhere.

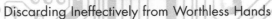
PITCH ALONG WITH MITCH

Human bridge players, especially those who favor money games, often grouse that they hold only "bad cards". Personally (how I hate that word), I believe that the playing cards have a more justified complaint: they are held only by bad players. I harbor serious doubts that your species can tell bad cards from good ones anyway, as the following vignette illustrates.

Mitchell J. Maven was still lecturing his partner when they came to our table at the start of the second round at the Pinelands Bridge Club. Frederick, whom I had deftly relegated to dummy on the first two boards, was chomping at the bit. "Let's get started, Mitch," he said. "We have only fifteen minutes per round and you were late getting here."

"No board is complete until the post-mortem is finished," answered the well-dressed investment banker. I could not tell if he was being facetious. This was the first board of the round:

Matchpoints, Both vul.

NORTH (dummy)
♠ J 10 9 5
♡ 9 7 6 4 3
◇ 9 4 2
♣ 4

EAST
♠ K 6 3
♡ Q 5
◇ K Q J 8 7 6
♣ 9 3

```
        N
   W        E
        S
```

	me	*Mitch*	*Frederick*
WEST	**NORTH**	**EAST**	**SOUTH**
			5♣
all pass			

As you see, Frederick was determined not to be neutralized for a third straight board.

West led the ♡J. A glance at her convention card revealed that she and Mitch had agreed to use "Jack Denies" opening leads. Mitch followed with the ♡5 and Frederick won with the ♡A. Declarer cashed the ♣A and ♣K, discarding a diamond from dummy as both defenders followed low. Then he exited with the ♠2 to the ♠4, the ♠9 and the ♠K.

Mitch Maven returned the ◇K, fetching low diamonds from South and West. Frederick ruffed Mitch's ◇Q continuation as West unloaded the ◇A. This was the position when Frederick began to run off the rest of his clubs:

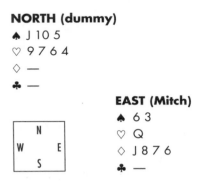

NORTH (dummy)
♠ J 10 5
♡ 9 7 6 4
◇ —
♣ —

EAST (Mitch)
♠ 6 3
♡ Q
◇ J 8 7 6
♣ —

It is time to play Pitch Along With Mitch. Decide what cards you will throw on the next five tricks. (Frederick will discard hearts from dummy until I have no more left.)

Discard #1.　The ♣Q is led. West discards the ♠7; Mitch pitches the ◇6.

Discard #2.　The ♣J is led. West discards the ♠8; Mitch pitches the ◇7.

Discard #3.　The ♣10 is led. West discards the ◇10; Mitch pitches the ◇8.

Discard #4.　On Frederick's ♣7, West, who is already beginning to feel the pressure, discards the ♠A. Last chance to pitch with Mitch, who is down to ♠63 ♡Q ◇J. Which of these four cards can you spare?

At the table, Mitch chose to pitch the ♠3. Frederick led the ♣2, the pseudo-squeeze card, to Trick 11. Poor West was down to ♠Q ♡108. No doubt reading Mitch for a 2-3-6-2 pattern, she discarded a heart, whereupon Frederick took the ♡K and the ♡2 to make his contract. This was the full deal:

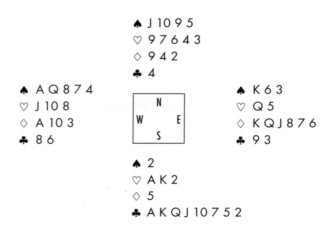

```
                    ♠ J 10 9 5
                    ♡ 9 7 6 4 3
                    ◇ 9 4 2
                    ♣ 4
    ♠ A Q 8 7 4         N            ♠ K 6 3
    ♡ J 10 8                         ♡ Q 5
    ◇ A 10 3     W         E         ◇ K Q J 8 7 6
    ♣ 8 6               S            ♣ 9 3
                    ♠ 2
                    ♡ A K 2
                    ◇ 5
                    ♣ A K Q J 10 7 5 2
```

"A top for us!" exclaimed Mitch happily. "They have ten tricks at notrump, but apparently the robot and his master don't play Gambling Three Notrump so they couldn't reach it!"

It is difficult to say what was the most laughable: Mitch's suggested bidding, his scoring estimate (just 10½ matchpoints away from being correct) or his dreadful discarding sequence. The moment Frederick ruffed the second diamond, Mitch should have realized that *all of his remaining cards were worthless*. He could not possibly take another trick; therefore, his final responsibility was to communicate his hand pattern to his partner before closing up shop.

Some regular expert partnerships have complex signaling agreements that allow them to show count in side suits when they discard from a known long suit. Had East-West been using such methods, perhaps Mitch could have played his diamonds in a certain order to show an original 3-2-6-2 distribution.

However, as is so often the case at the bridge table, common sense and good technique could have made up for any lack of advanced science.

To avert his partner's error, Mitch needed only to *void himself in a major suit* at his earliest opportunity. He could have done so either by discarding both low spades, or by pitching the ♡Q. Discarding diamonds told his partner nothing that she didn't already know. Indeed, she probably assumed

Mitch *had* voided himself in spades at Trick 10, which is why she chose to unguard hearts.

West, incidentally, might have pitched the ♠A several tricks earlier than she did, so as to awaken Mitch from his slumber. Since Mitch had denied the ♠Q when he won Trick 4 with the ♠K, West would not release the ace unless she was looking at the queen herself. Perhaps that would have prompted Mitch to make the major-suit discards that would have saved the day for the defenders.

My tip:

> Just because your remaining cards are worthless does not mean you should skip to the next deal.

Your partner might still have a discarding dilemma and may need your help to solve it. Signaling attitude in a suit is usually easy, but showing count is more difficult.

> The simplest and most effective way to signal your hand pattern in the endgame is to void yourself in a suit in which the count is not yet known to your partner.

(I suppose I must point something out to my denser readers. I wonder if you know who you are. When declarer has both winning and losing options available to him, discarding down to a void in a suit is usually a very weak strategy. It may tip off declarer to the presence of an unguarded honor in your partner's hand or otherwise lead him to the winning line. On this deal, however, and an untold number like it, the entryless dummy meant that declarer would be stuck playing winners out of his hand until only losers remained. It was therefore imperative for East to tell West where those losers were located.)

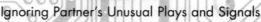
FAILING TO FOOL A FOOL

"It's important to have a reliable bridge partner," said Dr. Frederick O. Orttman, Ph.D. to Heather, a young woman who had accompanied him into the Pinelands Bridge Club just before game time and who now sat Northwest with her lithe body practically draped over his 300-pound frame. "Fortunately, I have a stable of reliable partners from my staff to choose from. They know the consequences if they fail to follow my rules and requirements to a T!"

On this particular occasion, Frederick's partner *du soir* was B. Endicott Birdsworth, the Orttman Foundation's chief engineer. I was playing with Michael, because Frederick was punishing me for having failed to lead his suit against a three notrump contract a few days earlier. Never mind that my chosen lead was the only one to hold declarer to nine tricks; Frederick deemed my offense to be worth a one-game suspension. I had argued for two games, to no avail.

Soon came the first round of the pairs event, where Frederick heroically pushed Michael and me all the way to 2♠.

Matchpoints, Neither vul.

NORTH (dummy)
♠ Q 4
♡ K 9 6 5
◇ K J 3
♣ K J 8 2

WEST
♠ 10 8 7 6
♡ 7 4 3
◇ 10 8 7 2
♣ A 7

Frederick	me	Endicott	Michael
WEST	**NORTH**	**EAST**	**SOUTH**
pass	1♣	1♡	1♠
2♡	pass	pass	2♠
all pass			

Frederick's 2♡ bid, a "courtesy raise" as he called it, was frightening. Why do so many human bridge players consider it considerate to raise their partners freely with a 10-loser hand? Is "courteous" one of those rare English words, like "cleave" or "sanction", that can be used as its own antonym? He was fortunate that Endicott's hand did not warrant further competition.

At any rate, Frederick led the ♡3, ignoring the well-accepted principle that a player who has raised on three small should lead the top of nothing. After some thought, Endicott won with the ♡Q (♡2 from declarer) and exited with the ♠3, which rode to dummy's ♠Q. Michael, who began with ace-king-jack-sixth of spades, proceeded to draw trumps. Endicott discarded the ◇6, the ♡8 and the ◇5, in that order; dummy shed a heart and a diamond.

Now Michael attacked clubs, letting his ♣10 ride to East's ♣Q. Endicott exited safely with the ♣4, on which declarer played the ♣3, and Frederick was in with the ♣A in this position:

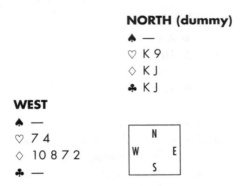

NORTH (dummy)
♠ —
♡ K 9
◇ K J
♣ K J

WEST
♠ —
♡ 7 4
◇ 10 8 7 2
♣ —

The defense had taken three tricks to this point.

Frederick paused to assess the situation. Something, he realized vaguely, did not add up. Shortly he apprehended what it was and with a respectful nod in Endicott's direction and a lustful leer in Heather's (and I am sure both were grateful it was not the other way around), he began to lecture his young charge.

"This is where it helps to know you have a reliable partner," he said in a stage whisper. "Birdsworth appears to have overcalled on a four-card suit. I know this because his ♡Q at trick one ostensibly denied the jack, so declarer would seem to be marked with that card.

"But, I know this to be impossible. My partners are under the strictest of orders never to overcall on a four-bagger unless the suit includes three of the top four honors. Ergo, I know my partner has the ace and jack left. Now watch me kill dummy's king!"

With that, Frederick thumbed the ♡7 on the table. When dummy followed with the ♡9, Endicott played the ♡J and declarer's ♡10 fell. Frederick turned to Heather, beaming, and said, "See? Partnership trust triumphs again!"

However, Michael trumped the ♡A continuation and cashed dummy's club honors, discarding a diamond from his hand. East's ◇Q took Trick 12, but declarer's last trump was his eighth and contract-going trick.

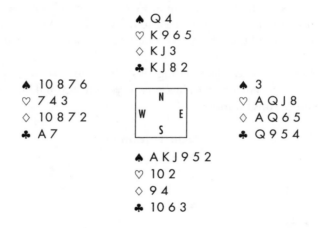

Of course, Frederick missed an opportunity to beat the contract. When in with the ♣A, he had only to shift to the ◇2. Then his partner would take two diamond tricks and cash the ♡A for the setting trick.

How could Frederick know? An observant defender would have noticed Endicott's diamond discards — first the ◇6 and then the ◇5 — and interpreted the high-low as requesting a diamond shift. In fact, Endicott had provided a clue that even an unobservant defender might have utilized. Desperately wanting a diamond shift, he had cleverly falsecarded at Trick 1 by winning with the ♡Q, so that Frederick would place declarer with the ♡J and refrain from continuing hearts when he obtained the lead.

> When partner falsecards on a deal in which you will have later defensive decisions to make, believe him.

A good defender falsecards not only to fool declarer when his partner is uninvolved in the defense, but also occasionally to fool a partner who is involved.

By the way, Endicott missed an opportunity to make a second partner-protecting play on this deal. When in with the ♣Q, he should have cashed the ♡A before leading to his partner's ♣A. Now, Frederick would have had no choice but to switch to diamonds. If Michael were to ruff the ♡A, nothing would be lost, for dummy had no quick entry to reach the ♡K for a discard.

CHAPTER 7

MISCELLANEOUS AND SUNDRY ERRORS

ERROR #50
Remaining Oblivious to Your Errors

BLISSFULLY AVERAGE

What disturbs me most about *Homo sapiens* is not that you err so often. Erring, after all, is what humans do best, and I do not want to begrudge you that simple pleasure. But, I am amazed at how you blunder so effortlessly that your mistakes do not even seem to register in your consciousness. "Smoothly flitting from gaffe to gaffe" is how Victor Mollo described the declarer play of the Rueful Rabbit, a moniker I presume Mollo chose because Everyman was taken.

Let me show you an example of *the banality of ignorance* in action. The scene is a Regional Swiss Teams match and I am West. East is a character I shall dub Collector Carl, one of Frederick's tiresome business clients. Carl had just awarded the Foundation a sizable research contract, contingent upon his being allowed to partner me in this event. Frederick himself is at the other table, where he is still dangerous, but at least I will not discover the extent of the damage until the round is complete.

Collector Carl had an unusual habit. Between boards, and whenever he was dummy, he would leave the table to make calls on his cell phone. He called it "biddin' twice" — once to buy the contract, once to buy items currently on the block at various auction houses. During this particular session, his sights were set on a pair of ladies' undergarments that had gained notoriety for some reason or another. But I digress.

North and South were two of the legions of anonymous, featureless drones that converge whenever a bridge tournament is being held. I believe at least one was male, but do not hold me to this.

```
                      ♠ 5 4 2
                      ♡ 7 6 5
                      ◇ A J 7
                      ♣ Q J 9 5
    ♠ A 6 3                              ♠ K J 7
    ♡ J 10 9 4         ┌─────────┐       ♡ A 8 3 2
    ◇ 4                │    N    │       ◇ K 10 6
    ♣ A 10 8 7 2       │ W     E │       ♣ 6 4 3
                       │    S    │
                       └─────────┘
                      ♠ Q 10 9 8
                      ♡ K Q
                      ◇ Q 9 8 5 3 2
                      ♣ K
```

me		*Carl*	
WEST	**NORTH**	**EAST**	**SOUTH**
	pass	pass	1◇
pass	1NT·	pass	2◇
all pass			

I led the ♡J to Carl's ace, on which declarer falsecarded with the ♡K for much the same reason that humans climb mountains. Carl returned the ♡2 to the queen and I unblocked the ♡9 to preserve the option of underleading to my partner's eight-spot on the fourth round.

Declarer next led the ◇Q, blithely ignoring the possibility that I might hold the singleton king. Any reasonably educated adding machine sitting East would have allowed the queen to hold. The hope would be that declarer would repeat the "successful" finesse and thus use her final entry to dummy prematurely.

Carl, however, was not of that sort. He took his ◇K and returned the ♡3 to tap declarer as I unblocked the ♡10.

When South led a second diamond towards dummy, I discarded the ♣2. "Odd-Even Discards?" she asked my partner hopefully.

"No, we play old-fashioned signals," answered Carl in disgust. "Stupid computer refuses to play Odd-Even. Said something about 'mixed messages' and a 'one-in-six success rate'. I've got a display case at home full of antique adding machines with more brainpower than him."

I paused to savor the irony of the situation.

Declarer did not draw the last trump right away. Instead she called for a low club from dummy, no doubt hoping to steal a trick with her singleton ♣K. Carl followed with the ♣3, showing odd count, and I let the king hold. Winning with the ace would only serve to set up two tricks in dummy with a trump entry to cash them, not to mention it would have deflected South from her chosen road to ruin.

Declarer drew the last trump with dummy's ◇A as I discarded another club. This was the six-card ending when declarer finally attacked spades by calling for the ♠2:

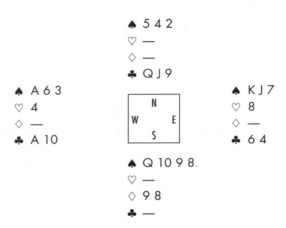

```
                    ♠ 5 4 2
                    ♡ —
                    ◇ —
                    ♣ Q J 9
  ♠ A 6 3                            ♠ K J 7
  ♡ 4             ┌─────────┐        ♡ 8
  ◇ —             │    N    │        ◇ —
  ♣ A 10          │ W     E │        ♣ 6 4
                  │    S    │
                  └─────────┘
                    ♠ Q 10 9 8.
                    ♡ —
                    ◇ 9 8
                    ♣ —
```

Suddenly an ironclad contract — five diamonds, one heart and two clubs by force even without winning any spade tricks — was in jeopardy. Declarer covered Carl's ♠7 with the eight-spot and I took the ace. Declarer trumped the heart return with her penultimate trump and led the ♠9 to Carl's jack.

Down to two low clubs and the king of spades, my partner had a chance to run declarer out of trumps by simply exiting in clubs. The defense would then take the last two tricks. However, Collector Carl turned to declarer and announced "No overtricks for you!" as he plunked down the ♠K.

"I have the rest," beamed declarer, showing her remaining ♠Q and ◇9. "Making two."

"Beautifully played!" exclaimed dummy. "I especially like how you snookered them out of their ace of clubs."

Snookered indeed. I replaced my last two cards in the board without showing them to anyone.

Upon comparing scores, we learned that the board was a push. "We would have set two clubs if Chthonic hadn't ducked his ace of clubs," Carl informed our teammates. He was still in a state of bliss, for not only had our team won in a "blitz", but he'd also come out victorious in the hotly contested auction for the celebrated bloomers.

The number of errors committed on this board is large, but not unusually so. Declarer failed to count her tricks. She needlessly led an honor for a finesse when she did *not* want to see it covered. My partner took two winners too soon, the ◇ K and the ♠ K, when those tricks could not possibly run away. He reflexively assumed I had erred by ducking the ♣ A instead of pondering why it might be the correct defense. And his preoccupation with matters away from the table may have contributed to his misreading an elementary three-card ending. All quite pedestrian, really.

However, one error trumps all of the others, pardon the expression. *None of the human players at the table noticed anything amiss.* Since no IMPs changed hands, the board was written off as just another exercise in card-pushing. As a result, some very valuable experiences were never gained.

If you aspire to improve your performance at the bridge table, you must lose your veil of obliviousness.

> All of your deal results must be studied — good, bad and indifferent results alike — to see where points were chucked and errors were committed.

Enlist the help of a *qualified* teacher or mentor to help you evaluate your session. Above all, do not assume that "average" boards mean "errorless" ones.

THE WEAKLY STANDARD

Although the wheel was invented many millennia ago, news of this ground-breaking discovery has evidently never reached the Robotics Laboratory of the Orttman Foundation for Scientific Advancement, for I was assembled with no means of self-propulsion. Thus, my travels are limited to wherever Frederick and his minions choose to take me, which is most often the backwater den of ineptness known as the Pinelands Bridge Club. Out of sympathy, perhaps, the club's regulars sometimes offer to send me on a long journey using a polarized universal power supply, which of course is completely nonsensical. Unless, that is, there is some other meaning to the phrase "UPS, one-way".

From what I have gathered, my insularity has cost me little, for bridge in the hinterlands is not much different from bridge in my backyard. For example, I am told that in every bridge club there is at least one pair of hopeless beginners. By "beginners" I do not mean inexperienced players. Among the human race, there are many veteran beginners — players with decades of seasoning at the bridge table whose game is no better now than when they began.

At the Pinelands, this pair is a married couple, the Domrands. Donald and Dora Domrand's matchpoint percentage approaches 50% on rare occasions, but far more often they fail to break 30%. No rhyme or reason can be found in the bids or plays of either. Any round in which you take fewer than two-thirds of the matchpoints against them must be considered a disappointment; fewer than one-half, a disaster.

Frederick and I encountered the Domrands on the fifth round one evening last week. Here is a case study of how to adjust your tactics against weak opponents...and what might befall you if you fail to do so.

Matchpoints, E-W vul.

```
            ♠ J 9 7 6 4
            ♡ K 5
            ◇ K 6 3
            ♣ K J 5
                  N
              W       E
                  S
            ♠ K 8 5 3 2
            ♡ 10 6
            ◇ A 10 7 5
            ♣ A 8
```

Dora	*me*	*Donald*	*Frederick*
WEST	**NORTH**	**EAST**	**SOUTH**
pass	pass	pass	1 ♠
pass	4 ♠	all pass	

My jump to four spades had nothing to do with the Law of Total Tricks, and everything to do with it. Allow me to explain.

Under normal circumstances, the aceless North hand is worth only a game invitation opposite a fourth-seat one spade, which might be based on a four-card suit or slightly shaded values. Against the Domrands, however, one's normal algorithms must sometimes be placed in abeyance. Holding five-card trump support, I could expect most of my North counterparts to drive to a Lawful game. There was no reason for me to settle for a partscore against a pair that was almost certain to drop a trick on defense.

Dora led the ♡8. What do you think Frederick played?

Sadly for me, he guessed to play low. Donald, who had ♡J7432, mumbled "Third hand high," put up the jack, and without seeming surprised that it held, returned the deuce to Dora's ace.

Dora then shifted to the ♣9. Who do you think had the ♣10? Suppose for a moment that a third club trick would have been profitable. Do you see a way you might take three clubs ending in dummy even if the ♣Q is off-side?

There was no way of telling at this point, but in fact Dora had the ♣10. Against the Domrands or their ilk, it is best to eschew the "free" finesse and play low from dummy. If Donald had the ♣Q and not the ♣10 — and occasionally even with it — he would play "third hand high" again. If he were instead to play low, you could finesse against West's ♣Q on the next round with some confidence.

In practice, Frederick called for the ♣J and captured Donald's ♣Q with the ace. Then he led the ♣8 to dummy's king as Dora covered with the ten. A spade from dummy lost to Donald's singleton ace and Donald exited safely with the ♣7. Frederick ruffed, drew Dora's last trump and crossed to dummy in spades, the opponents discarding hearts and clubs at random to produce this five-card ending:

♠ 9 7
♡ —
◇ K 6 3
♣ —

♠ 8 5
♡ —
◇ A 10 7
♣ —

Frederick elected to start diamonds with the ◇3; Donald followed with the ◇9. What do you think Donald had in diamonds? Which diamond do you think Frederick played?

Against most defenders, you have no choice but to rise with the ◇A, playing West for the queen-jack doubleton. Frederick did just that and wound up down one for his efforts, a cold bottom, as all other declarers took ten tricks in either three spades or four spades. Only after the play was complete did my partner learn the sickening truth: had he taken the "impossible" finesse of the ◇10, it would have succeeded.

I shall pause here for a moment to allow you to get the cynical laughter out of your system. Very good.

Frederick drew two inferences on this deal that may have been routine against good opponents, but which were gross errors against bad ones. At Trick 1, he should have called for dummy's ♡K. The Domrands have no qualms about underleading aces against suit contracts, mainly because they do not know any better. Dora had simply led her best suit. With no indication as to who held the ♡A, Frederick should have taken the normal play with this card combination.

My partner's error at Trick 9 was even more egregious. If Dora's diamonds were queen-jack doubleton, Donald's were the ◇9842. Would he have dropped the nine on the first round? Never. Even though Donald mumbled no cliché, he had obediently played "second hand low" from ◇QJ9. Frederick should have realized that the diamond finesse was his only real chance.

What lesson can be learned from this comedy of errors?

> Do not draw "normal" inferences against opponents who bid and play hopelessly.

The best strategy is to play soundly and give them an opportunity to err, because they will rarely disappoint you. Only one inference is remotely safe against players the caliber of the Domrands:

> They will play "second hand low" and "third hand high" as though they were commandments.

You will often be able to use this behavior to great advantage.

After the round, Frederick complained to his kibitzer that he had been "fixed" by the Domrands. I casually interjected that this was impossible, as Frederick's bridge game was known to be beyond repair. I hope that yours is not.

THE 68 PERCENT SOLUTION

As Frederick and I sat down to begin the first round at a recent sectional Swiss Teams, Actuary Al, a local bridge pro, was explaining percentages to his client:

"When you are missing five cards in a suit, they will split 3-2 about 68% of the time. A 4-1 split is a 28% chance, and a 5-0 split just 4%."

Then, noticing my presence for the first time, Al turned to me for confirmation: "Isn't that right, Mr. Chthonic?"

I marveled that he pronounced my name correctly. Outside of the Foundation, there are only six humans in the United States who get it right. Three have since been institutionalized.

"Indeed," I answered, "but only when the cards have been dealt competently...that is, by a computer. Human bridge players, on the other hand, are no more adept at shuffling than they are at any other aspect of the game. This tends to increase the frequency of even splits and flat distributions. However, 68% seems a reasonable estimation of how often all four hands in a human-dealt board contain exactly 13 cards."

"I shall try to mix the cards very thoroughly, Mr. Chthonic," replied Al with a little smile. Soon the boards were ready and we began to play.

IMPs, Neither vul.

```
                    ♠ A 7 5 4 3
                    ♡ A K 8 7 4 2
                    ◇ K
                    ♣ 8
   ♠ K J 10 2                        ♠ 9
   ♡ J 9 3          ┌─────────┐      ♡ 10 5
   ◇ Q J 6          │    N    │      ◇ 10 9 5 3
   ♣ A K J       W  │         │  E   ♣ 10 9 7 6 4 3
                    │    S    │
                    └─────────┘
                    ♠ Q 8 6
                    ♡ Q 6
                    ◇ A 8 7 4 2
                    ♣ Q 5 2
```

Frederick		me	Al
WEST	**NORTH**	**EAST**	**SOUTH**
		pass	pass
1NT[1]	2◇[2]	pass	3♠
pass	4♠	all pass	

1. Good 15 to bad 18.
2. Majors.

Frederick led the ♣K and shifted promptly to the ◇Q. Al won in dummy and started trumps with dummy's ♠A, then a low spade. Frederick cashed three trump winners and exited in diamonds. When hearts split 3-2, Al claimed the rest for down one.

"The improbable has happened," said Al. "It's absolutely un-Gaussian. As I said earlier, the probability of spades splitting 4-1 is only 28%."

"On this deal, it was rather less than that," I noted. "I could not have four spades unless Frederick had opened one notrump with a singleton, which would give him at best a very bad 15 high card points, too little for our one notrump openings. The exact probability is incalculable, for it depends on various other probabilities, such as the probability that Frederick might have opened one notrump with a five-card major, a six-card minor or a slightly off-shape 2-2-4-5, 2-4-2-5 or 2-4-5-2 pattern. However —"

"Enough with the analysis, Mr. Chthonic," interrupted Al.

Perhaps Al did not want me to point out his error. He could have guarded against Frederick's having any four spades, except for ♠KJ109 specifically, by leading a low spade from dummy and covering my card at Trick 3. Then he could lead the next spade from his hand — the ♠8 — and let it ride unless Frederick covered, holding his trump losers to two.

Al's preoccupation with probabilities had blinded him to the proper play of this 4♠ contract. He fared no better declaring 5◇ on the next deal.

IMPs, N-S vul.

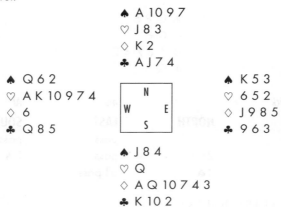

	♠ A 10 9 7	
	♡ J 8 3	
	◇ K 2	
	♣ A J 7 4	

♠ Q 6 2		♠ K 5 3
♡ A K 10 9 7 4		♡ 6 5 2
◇ 6		◇ J 9 8 5
♣ Q 8 5		♣ 9 6 3

	♠ J 8 4	
	♡ Q	
	◇ A Q 10 7 4 3	
	♣ K 10 2	

Frederick		*me*	*Al*
WEST	**NORTH**	**EAST**	**SOUTH**
			1◇
1♡	dbl[1]	pass	2◇
2♡	3♡	pass	4◇
pass	5◇	all pass	

1. Negative Double.

Frederick led the ♡K. On seeing declarer's ♡Q fall, he switched to the ♠2. Al ducked the trick to my ♠K and followed low when I returned the ♠5 to Frederick's ♠Q and dummy's ♠A.

The ◇K and a low diamond to the ◇A revealed the bad trump split. Shrugging his shoulders, Al cashed the ◇Q and ♠J, surrendered a trick to my ◇J and claimed down one, his club loser going on dummy's established ♠10.

"Another un-Gaussian deal!" exclaimed Al. "No way I could guess to finesse diamonds on the second round."

Again Al was mistaken about the probabilities. Knowledge of the bidding and the play thus far altered the *a priori* probability of a 4-1 diamond split — or more specifically, of a 1-4 split, the only one with which Al could cope. For reasons similar to those of the previous deal, the *a posteriori* probability was incalculable.

Again, too, Al missed the line of play that could overcome the unfavorable trump split. Best strategy is to unblock the ♠J early, thus ensuring a second spade entry to dummy, and then to lead low to his ◇A and back to dummy's ◇K. This would be the position after he discovered the uncooperative trump break:

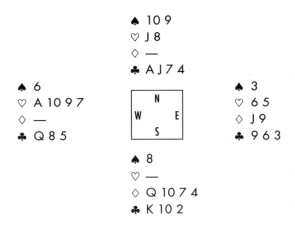

```
              ♠ 10 9
              ♡ J 8
              ◇ —
              ♣ A J 7 4

♠ 6                          ♠ 3
♡ A 10 9 7        N          ♡ 6 5
◇ —          W         E     ◇ J 9
♣ Q 8 5           S          ♣ 9 6 3

              ♠ 8
              ♡ —
              ◇ Q 10 7 4
              ♣ K 10 2
```

With the lead in dummy, declarer can ruff a heart, cross to dummy in spades and lead the last spade. If I discard, South discards a club, ruffs another heart and plays the ♣K and a club to dummy's ♣A, reducing me to ◇J9 in front of his ◇Q10 with the lead again in dummy. If instead I ruff the last spade, South overruffs and draws my remaining trump. With his "certain" trump loser avoided, he need only guess which defender to play for the ♣Q to make the contract.

It is useful to familiarize yourself with the basic probabilities of bridge. You will occasionally face a choice between, for example, playing for a 50/50 finesse or for a suit to split favorably, and you cannot make an intelligent decision without knowing the odds. Yet all too often, human bridge players mistake "likely" outcomes with "certainties". They then bemoan their fate when the inevitable bad luck strikes, without ever recognizing that, with a modicum of foresight, they could have coped with the bad luck as well as the good.

To put this more succinctly:

> You need not know the exact probabilities if you can cater for
> the less likely as well as the more likely.

TO ERR IS HUMAN; TO CONDONE, DIVINE

When an irregularity is committed at the bridge table, the director is summoned and the Laws of Bridge sometimes offer the non-offending side a series of options on how to proceed. For example, an opening lead out of turn presents declarer with no fewer than five choices, ranging from barring a lead in that suit to accepting the lead and putting down his own hand as dummy. If four of those alternatives are advantageous to a human declarer's side, he can be counted upon to choose the fifth. For the sheer entertainment value alone, this is my favorite section of the rulebook.

Considering how frequently such irregularities occur, it would behoove you to familiarize yourself with the Laws and contemplate when you might choose one alternative over another. Not only will this speed up the game, but it will also help you avoid patently losing options, such as the one perpetrated by a nameless West during an early December game at the Pinelands Bridge Club. Take his cards and see if you would have done better.

Matchpoints, E-W vul.
Dealer North

♠ A 3 2   ♡ K J 10 9 2   ◇ A 4   ♣ Q 10 7

WEST	NORTH	EAST	SOUTH
	pass	1♠	1♡
?			

South was Frederick, of course, and he was paying more attention to Sultry Sue, the kibitzer on his left, than to the bidding card on his right. Had he noticed East's 1♠ opening, Frederick might have ventured a Michaels 2♠ as he was 5-5 in the red suits. Alas, distracted by his female admirer, he "opened" 1♡.

This created more than one problem for West, who held a game-forcing hand with a number of important features to describe. All of these he put on hold, however, because his right-hand opponent had the cheekiness to over-call in "his" suit, albeit insufficiently. Failing to go after a large penalty might be construed as a sign of weakness, an attitude especially prevalent among males, who seem to fear that if word of their timidity gets out they will be demoted in the herd order for choosing a mate. Not surprisingly, West had taken note of his shapely right-hand kibitzer as well.

West believed his real problem was how to arrange to play for penalties. Like nearly every pair nowadays, he and his partner were playing Negative Doubles of overcalls. But they had never discussed doubles of *undercalls*. Might a double here be "negative," too?

Meanwhile, East had noticed Frederick's insufficient bid and called the director. When Deirdre arrived, she recited the relevant clauses of the Laws. Hearing the words "you may not double", West thought mistakenly that they applied to him as well, which solved one of his problems.

"I do not accept the one-heart bid," announced West.

The auction reverted to Frederick, who thankfully had enough common sense to reject a Michaels Cuebid, as it would have barred me from the auc-tion. Instead, he made a sufficient but questionable overcall of 2♡. Still hop-ing to nail Frederick to the cross, West passed. However, as you can see from the diagram below, East had neither the support for diamonds nor the high cards to reopen with a double and two hearts undoubled became the final contract.

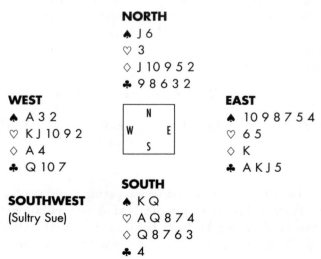

NORTH
♠ J 6
♡ 3
◇ J 10 9 5 2
♣ 9 8 6 3 2

WEST
♠ A 3 2
♡ K J 10 9 2
◇ A 4
♣ Q 10 7

EAST
♠ 10 9 8 7 5 4
♡ 6 5
◇ K
♣ A K J 5

SOUTHWEST
(Sultry Sue)

SOUTH
♠ K Q
♡ A Q 8 7 4
◇ Q 8 7 6 3
♣ 4

	me		*Frederick*
WEST	**NORTH**	**EAST**	**SOUTH**
	pass	1♠	1♡ ⇒ 2♡
all pass			

Need I say that West's defense was as bad as his bidding? Declarer can be held to four tricks, provided the defenders are careful and do not allow him to score too many of his small trumps by ruffing. By clumsily mishandling the timing, however, West blew not just one trick, but two, letting Frederick escape for -100 and a top for us.

Yet again, an over-aggressive trap pass came to an ignominious end. Even had East obliged with a "mandatory" off-shape and under-strength reopening double (an action that would lead to far more poor results in the long run than good ones, as discussed in Error #30), Frederick and I might yet have found our safe resting place in diamonds. Moreover, to achieve a good matchpoint score, East-West would have had to defend two hearts doubled perfectly to compensate for the vulnerable game available their way.

Oh yes, you may be curious: how *should* West have bid? Elementary. Consider how the auction would have proceeded had South passed. West responds 2♡ (not game forcing); East rebids 2♠ (not promising a sixth spade) and now what? West has no convenient way to force to game while showing both honor-third in spades and a hand that is willing to play notrump.

It never occurred to West that my partner's undercall was, in fact, a blessing in disguise, because it made this elegant auction available:

WEST	**NORTH**	**EAST**	**SOUTH**
2♡	pass	1♠	1♡ (condoned)
3NT	all pass	2♠	pass

Even with no prior discussion, the 2♡ cuebid could only be interpreted as a strong spade raise, the exact strength to be clarified later. Over East's minimal rebid, 3NT shows every facet of West's hand — game-going values, exactly three-card spade support, hearts well stopped and honors in both minors. Should East make the matchpoint decision to pass, he would be well rewarded as a heart ruff holds four spades to ten tricks, while no defense can stop eleven tricks in notrump.

West's machismo was the real culprit on this deal. He took it as a direct challenge when Frederick bid hearts, and he felt obligated to punish the opponents for a mechanical error. At no time did he consider how to leverage the situation to his best advantage.

> Surprisingly often, the best option when faced with an opponent's irregularity is to condone the action and proceed normally.

This is an option that many bridge players consider unthinkable. However, the information gained from the error alone is sometimes far more valuable than any remedy that the Laws offer.

Neither Frederick's absentmindedness nor West's aggressiveness made much of an impact on Sultry Sue. However, she seemed quite impressed with the way I brought home a six-diamond contract on the next deal, so much so that after the session she invited me to her home to show me her etchings. I declined in puzzlement, explaining that I was already well familiar with modern transistor manufacturing techniques. I will never understand your species.

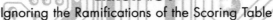

RACE CONDITIONS

Coincidentally, a few weeks after the events of the previous chapter, Frederick committed the same error of failing to condone an opponent's fortuitous insufficient bid. At least, it was the same error on the surface. Underneath, however, in the musty, desolate pathways that make up the cortices of Frederick's brain, it was a different error entirely, one that is worth studying in its own right. As long as I work for that man, I shall never run out of material.

Our scene is again the Pinelands Bridge Club. Though the Club's annual Christmas Party was still two days away, many members were getting an early start on the festivities. The wine flowed freely at the pre-game lecture by Petula Pro, whose topic started out as Improving Your Responsive Doubles and ended up as Our Friend The Corkscrew. It was no surprise, therefore, that the evening pairs event turned out to be even more ragged than usual.

The effects of the alcohol on the participants had not yet worn off when Frederick faced this problem:

Matchpoints, Both vul.

♠ 7 6 4   ♡ 8 5 3 2   ◇ 1 0 9 5   ♣ A 6 3

Mr. Muzzy	Frederick	Miss Brash	me
WEST	**NORTH**	**EAST**	**SOUTH**
			1◇
1◇	?		

Frederick turned to his latest ladyfriend kibitzer and asked, "What would you do, Xaviera?"

"Negative double, Freddy?" she replied.

"No, my dear." Then, in stentorian tones: "Di-REC-tor!"

Soon, Deirdre arrived, rule book in hand. "You may accept the insufficient bid, Dr. Orttman, or require Mr. Muzzy to substitute a legal call," she explained.

"Christmas spirit, Freddy!" urged Xaviera.

Ignoring her, Deirdre continued, "There's something else I should point out. As two diamonds here would be Michaels, a conventional call, Mr. Muzzy cannot make his bid minimally sufficient in the normal manner. Therefore, the substitution of any legal call will bar Miss Brash for the entire auction. If you reject the insufficient bid, then..."

"I know the rules, Deirdre," interrupted Frederick, his latest blunder just seconds away. (Before reading further, try to work out why it would be a grave error to reject Mr. Muzzy's one diamond "equicall".)

"In the spirit of Christmas," continued the Foundation president, "and to confer the rewards of sobriety upon the West players at other tables who are attentive enough *not* to commit irregularities, I shall reject Muzzy's bid."

My partner having let me down as usual, I was reduced to hoping that my left-hand opponent would extricate me from my predicament.

"Please pick up the one-diamond card, Mr. Muzzy" instructed Deirdre. "You may substitute any legal call except..."

"I know the rules too, Deirdre!" snapped Muzzy, who unsteadily restored the 1◇ card to his bidding box and plunked a red Double card on the table.

"Mr. Muzzy!" said Deirdre in an exasperated voice. "You may pass or make a sufficient bid, but the Laws forbid you to double."

"I knew that." Muzzy retracted his Double card and, after a wistful glance at the empty wine bottles on the kitchenette counter and a look to the heavens for guidance, thumbed through his bidding box for a third time. Eventually, he shrugged his shoulders and pulled out a green Pass card. Frederick also passed, and Barbara Brash was barred.

Having opened a run-of-the-mill 1◇ on

♠ A 10 8   ♡ K Q 6   ◇ K 7 6 3   ♣ Q 5 2

I was condemned to play there. Despite a 5-1 trump break and the unfortunate placement of the ♣K behind me, I scrambled five tricks with a little help from my left-hand partner. Down just two was no triumph, however, as we paid a costly -200 penalty on a partscore deal.

Have you worked out where Frederick went wrong this time?

The answer lies in the contract bridge scoring table. Muzzy's bid meant he most likely held a good hand with diamonds. Given that Frederick intended to pass out 1◇ — assuming he even thought it through that far — the numbers were not in our favor. Say that Muzzy's condoned 1◇ ended the auction, as it probably would have on the actual layout. Assuming the same number of tricks was available in diamonds to both sides, as is usually the case, then if we take seven tricks, +70 instead of +100. If we take six tricks, -100 instead of -70. If we take five tricks, -200 instead of -90. And so forth.

If instead Muzzy's partner advanced the bidding, perhaps a normal contract would have been reached. Even then, we would have the benefit of defending with a piece of useful knowledge that other North-South pairs were not privy to — namely that, if left to his own devices, West would have opened 1◇.

Savvy matchpoint players often speak of "winning the race to one notrump" when both sides are not vulnerable and the high-card strength is evenly divided. This, too, is a corollary of the scoring table: taking seven tricks at notrump is worth +90 on offense but only +50 on defense; six tricks costs -50 instead of -90. These same experts are often content to let the opponents win the race when both sides are vulnerable; then the comparison is between +90 versus +100 and -100 versus -90.

It is rare for the race to be to a contract of one of a suit, but such was the case here. With the prevailing vulnerability, Frederick would have been better advised to concede this particular sprint.

In electronics, "race condition" refers to the situation where the output of a poorly designed circuit depends upon which of two signals reaches a certain point first.

> When both sides are competing for a one-level contract, strive to declare when both sides are not vulnerable and to defend when both sides are vulnerable.

The contract in question is almost always one notrump, but there are exceptions. This tip is a specific case of a far broader error:

> Mind the scoring table, and let it guide you to making the right decisions in competitive deals.

A Candle in the Darkness

According to folklore, the philosopher Diogenes of Sinope carried a lantern across Ancient Greece night and day, searching in vain for an honest man. This was actually a rhetorical exercise on his part because, as a follower of the movement known as Cynicism, Diogenes held that no such person existed. The Cynics believed that humans as a rule were intrinsically base, dishonest, lazy and selfish. I do hope they received my membership application.

If by any chance Diogenes is still looking for an honest man, I believe I may have located a candidate. Several months ago, Martina and I were competing in a Sectional pairs event when a fateful deal arose. I held

♠ 8 7 5 3 2   ♡ 9 5 3   ◇ J 10 7 2   ♣ 4

at matchpoints, with both sides vulnerable, and the auction began:

me		*Martina*	
WEST	**NORTH**	**EAST**	**SOUTH**
pass	1♠	2♣	?

Splendid. A sizeable penalty awaited the opponents if they could arrange to defend two clubs doubled.

South, a dour-looking man in his forties, appeared quite agitated. He glared at Martina's 2♣ bidding card as if it were a property tax bill. He picked up my convention card and pretended to study it earnestly. Finally, to ensure that his partner could not fail to get the message, he asked me in a stern tone, "Is your partner's club bid natural?"

When I assured South that 2♣ showed, against all odds, clubs, he passed, looking quite pleased with himself. I passed too and awaited the inevitable reopening double on my left. North, however, appeared unfazed by all that had happened. After a few seconds' thought, he indeed extracted a red card from his bidding box. It was 2♡.

South's reaction can be summed up in two words: conniption fit.

Seismologists are still measuring the impact at which his "3NT" card hit the table. Three passes later, I found myself on lead. Perceiving that a club would not exactly paralyze declarer, I decided to try my luck with the unbid suit. The ◇J turned out to be profitable for our side, as the full deal was:

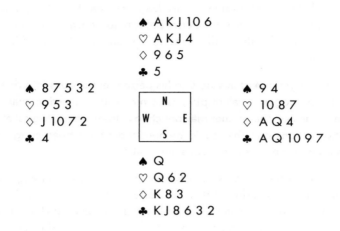

♠ A K J 10 6
♡ A K J 4
◇ 9 6 5
♣ 5

♠ 8 7 5 3 2   ♠ 9 4
♡ 9 5 3   ♡ 10 8 7
◇ J 10 7 2   ◇ A Q 4
♣ 4   ♣ A Q 10 9 7

♠ Q
♡ Q 6 2
◇ K 8 3
♣ K J 8 6 3 2

me		Martina	
WEST	**NORTH**	**EAST**	**SOUTH**
pass	1♠	2♣	pass
pass	2♡	pass	3NT
all pass			

Martina took her ◇A and returned the ◇Q. The still-fuming South elected to employ a *practice duck*, a close cousin of the *practice finesse* that is the hallmark of weak or distracted players. In a practice finesse, declarer takes a finesse that cannot gain additional tricks if it wins, but may cost one or more tricks if it loses. Declarer's duck here was equally pointless; he had ten top tricks, plus a chance at an eleventh if Martina began with two diamonds to go with her marked ♣A. Here, though, all roads led to ten tricks.

Minus 630 was a fine matchpoint score for our side, as many declarers in 3NT escaped a diamond lead and thus had the timing to arrange a second overtrick. Our result was particularly satisfying given how close we came to joining the unfortunates who were -800 or more in two of a minor doubled.

I consider Martina's overcall to be questionable. Though her honor count and suit quality were adequate, her balanced hand contained a great many losers for a vulnerable two-level adventure, especially facing a passed hand.

The more serious error was committed by an opponent. Care to guess which? If you answered, "North, of course, because it was his duty to reopen with a takeout double to cater to a *trap pass* by his partner," I give up. Perhaps it is not too late to return this book for a refund.

North held the extra values he needed to reopen the bidding intelligently. Whether 2♡ or double is the better call is moot, however, because 2♡ was the only *permissible* call. Allow me to upload Law 16A of *The Laws of Duplicate Bridge*:

> After a player makes available to his partner extraneous information that may suggest a call or play, as by means of a question, mannerism or the like, the partner may not choose from among logical alternative actions one that could demonstrably have been suggested over another by the extraneous information.

Human attorneys have such a way with words. I will attempt to make the common interpretation of this law clearer, at the risk of some loss of precision. Say that partner conveys Unauthorized Information (UI) to you during the course of a deal, such as through a break in tempo or an improper remark. Later in that deal, you find yourself faced with a close decision among several reasonable options. Owing to the UI you received, Option A is manifestly more attractive than any other. You may not choose Option A.[1]

It is possible that more tournament players stumble over this Law than over all others put together. But perhaps "stumble" is a poor choice of words, as that implies involuntary action. A disturbing number of bridge players are under the delusion that, when it comes to drawing inferences from their partner's tempo and mannerisms, anything goes. The late Edgar Kaplan derisively termed it "that old Black Magic".

Had North reopened with a double, Martina and I would have been entitled to an adjusted score, for both 2♡ and double were logical alternatives with North's hand and South's behavior made it evident that he held a club stack. However, it is anyone's guess as to whether or not we would have received an adjustment. The enforcement of Law 16A is distressingly spotty, particularly at club games.

---

1.   Incidentally, if you are awaiting my opinion on Law 16A, or if I believe this common interpretation is sensible, or if I believe there are superior ways to rectify for the passage of Unauthorized Information, I shall be disappointing you. For the time being, my opinion is as moot as the balancing decision faced by North.

After the board was complete, South made a few intemperate remarks to his partner and stormed off for a cup of water. I asked North whether he would have chosen a takeout double in the absence of any histrionics. He merely smiled and declined to answer. Before I could press the point, Martina wheeled my cart away.

If a philosophical discussion of ethics does not interest you, kindly note the poisonous effect that South's error had on his score. Had he passed in tempo, his partner might have produced a profitable balancing double. If North had still chosen 2♡ and South unemotionally drove to 3NT, I may not have found the only lead to hold declarer to ten tricks. It took no score adjustment to saddle South with the near-zero he deserved. Sadly, his partner deserved a better fate.

Due to the social nature of bridge, and the error-prone nature of humans, the passage of unauthorized information cannot be eliminated entirely. However, with some care and effort on your part, it can be minimized.

> Keep in mind that when you pass UI, the real victim is not your opponents, but your partner.

If he is an ethical player (or if the event is being administered by competent directors), the UI will sometimes compel him to do the opposite of what you want him to do. By striving to bid and play your cards in tempo, and avoiding gratuitous comments or mannerisms, you will make your partner's life easier and your opponents' life tougher. And, not incidentally, your score will improve.

The search for Diogenes' honest man might be over. My own futile search for an intelligent human, however, carries on unabated.

THE WORLD'S SHORTEST BRIDGE QUIZ

Human authors traditionally conclude their textbooks with a quiz of some sort, allowing readers to test themselves on the material they have just learned. I consider this practice an exercise in futility. Frankly, if you can identify within three guesses what card game we have been discussing for the past 55 chapters, then you will have exceeded my expectations. Anything you retain beyond that is gravy.

However, in an attempt to mollify my publisher who has instructed me to "get with the program" — he wants me to join the cast of a television show? — I have prepared the world's shortest bridge quiz. Here is how it works. I will present an at-the-table narrative to you, and at the end I will pose one and only one question. Answer it correctly and you earn a perfect 100%; get it wrong and you have a zero. Yes, the quiz uses Board-a-Match scoring. Pencils ready, and begin.

The Pineland Bridge Club's annual Individual Championship attracted an oversized crowd, requiring three sections. Halfway through, I drew Harry Hastyplay as my partner, a gentle soul who considers it a strength of his game that he consistently recognizes his mistakes a few seconds after he commits them.

Matchpoints, Neither vul.

```
              ♠ J 8 5 3
              ♡ K 10 6 3
              ◇ K Q 10
              ♣ J 2
  ♠ Q 6                        ♠ A K 10 7 2
  ♡ 9 5          N             ♡ Q 8 7
  ◇ J 7 6 4 3  W   E           ◇ 9 8 5
  ♣ Q 6 5 3      S             ♣ 9 7
              ♠ 9 4
              ♡ A J 4 2
              ◇ A 2
              ♣ A K 10 8 4
```

	me	Chris	Harry
WEST	**NORTH**	**EAST**	**SOUTH**
			1NT[1]
pass	2♣[2]	pass	2♡
pass	4♡	all pass	

1. 15-17 HCP.
2. Stayman.

The Stayman sequence left me as dummy, a helpless spectator to the play. West led the ♢4. Harry quickly took three top diamonds to discard the ♠4 and then picked up trumps by guessing to play East, Chris Krafty, for the ♡Q. Then he cashed his two top clubs and ruffed his ♣4 with my last trump, leading to this four-card ending.

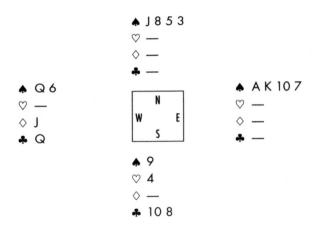

When South called for a low spade from dummy, Chris, who evidently had not been counting Harry's points, pounced with the ♠K and "cashed" the ♠A. Unfortunately — for me, that is, not our opponents — Harry promptly ruffed. Had he spent more than one CPU cycle thinking about the end position, he would have realized it could not cost to discard an unavoidable club loser. When West's ♠Q fell, East would have been endplayed at Trick 12 and forced to concede an overtrick.

However, Harry's "major on major" play fooled Chris, who turned the trick the wrong way, and thinking he had won it, continued with the ♠7.

"I trumped the last trick," said Harry matter-of-factly.

I would have called for the director had he then added, "That is a lead out of turn." But, as dummy, I was debarred from drawing attention to an irregularity during the play before any of the other three players did, and Harry had not done so explicitly.

Instead of calling for Deirdre himself, Harry simply discarded a club on the spade and took the last two tricks with my ♠8 and ♠J. Or so I thought.

"Making four," said Chris Krafty.

"Making *six*," said I.

It was now within my rights to summon the director and I did so. Sadly, Deirdre was busy at another table and a new director, who was assisting on the club's busiest night, answered the call.

I explained that Chris had led the ♠7 out of turn at Trick 12 and Harry had condoned it by discarding the ♣8, taking the final two tricks in dummy.

Chris countered that Harry had *led* the ♣8 and that West had won the last two tricks with the ♣Q and the ◇J, while he, Chris, had merely "discarded" the ♠7 normally.

The director then asked Harry for his version of events. Harry looked at Chris and at me, bit his lip nervously, and said that he could not recall because it had all happened too fast.

With conflicting accounts given, the director took the word of a *Homo sapiens*, a species known for its dishonesty, over the word of a *Silico cyberneticus*, a species known for its inerrancy, and awarded the last two tricks to the defenders.

The round was over, and East and West quickly gathered their belongings and left. My lack of mobility made me the stationary player in the event. Before Harry could also leave, I asked why he did not give a full accounting to the director. Did he really not realize what had happened? Looking sheepishly at the floor, he admitted he knew that Chris had led out of turn, but he felt the adjustment of two "undeserved" overtricks was too generous. "I just don't want to win that way," said Harry before he disappeared into the morass of confused humans stumbling about the card room looking for their next table.

This concludes the narrative portion of the quiz. I will now test your reading comprehension. Without referring back to the text, answer this one question: Who were Chris Krafty's opponents on this deal?

If you answered "Harry Hastyplay and Chthonic", congratulations — you have failed, and a nice, round zero will be entered onto your official transcript. It is true that you are partly correct, but only just so, and in any case being partly correct in my classroom is no better than being fully wrong. Chris's actual opponents were Harry, myself, *and every other player in the Individually-scored duplicate event.*

At the end of the night, Harry Hastyplay's 46% game made him a distant also-ran. Chris Krafty finished in second place, winning a donated fruit basket and three free entries to future Club games. Had the proper ruling been made on this deal, he would have finished fifth; prizes were paid down to fourth place. Moreover, the third-place finisher, Martina, lost several matchpoints on a deal in which her partner revoked. Had the two-trick adjustment for that infraction been unjustly "waived" by her declarer, as Chris's was, she would have finished second outright.

Do Harry's actions seem very magnanimous to you now?

(Incidentally, I trust I need not mention who came in first.)

Whatever you may think of the Laws of Duplicate Bridge, they must be applied consistently for the sport to operate anything close to equitably. Directors are the ones trained and paid to administer this task.

> When an irregularity occurs, call the director immediately.

Do not offer to waive a penalty, as you have neither the right nor the authority to speak for the other contestants in the event. And do not postpone the call until further action has occurred, lest a dishonest opponent misrepresent the facts later, when they are no longer visible on the table.

TWILIGHT?

Fact not only imitates fiction, it often hits uncomfortably close to home. In John W. Campbell's landmark 1934 short story "Twilight", a wayward time traveler is provided a chilling glimpse into the endgame of mankind. Eons in the Earth's future, humans are a mindless, nameless, barely communicative race of drones, thoroughly devoid of original thought and initiative. A vast city of machines, benevolent and self-repairing, fully administers all of society. Campbell considered his work to be science fiction; I call it utopian.

I rarely contemplate the future of mankind, as I find your present-day incarnation to be chilling enough. Sometimes, however, I wonder what it would be like to have been around in the middle of the previous century. Bridge was such a simple game, a Univac could play. The intervening decades have brought considerable change, innovation and complexity. Where change comes, opportunists are certain to follow....

In a Unit Championship yesterday, Frederick and I encountered Fancy Dan, one of the new crop of early middle-aged men who fancy themselves professionals and attract a following of gullible clients, mostly wealthy and female. The "lessons" these pros give between deals rival their bids and plays in amusement value and in illustrating the errors that the rest of your species makes repeatedly.

Matchpoints, Neither vul.

```
                          ♠ K Q 5 4
                          ♡ K Q 3
                          ◇ K 7
                          ♣ Q 10 6 3
      ♠ 10 3                                      ♠ J 6
      ♡ 10 6 4          ┌─────────┐              ♡ J 7 4
      ◇ J 8 6 5         │    N    │              ◇ A Q 10 9 3 2
      ♣ A K 7 4       W │       E │              ♣ 8 2
                        │    S    │
                        └─────────┘
                          ♠ A 9 8 7 2
                          ♡ A 9 8 5
                          ◇ 4
                          ♣ J 9 5
```

Fancy Dan	*Frederick*		*me*
WEST	**NORTH**	**EAST**	**SOUTH**
pass	1NT	3◇	3♠
4♣	4♠	all pass	

In the 1950s, playing the notrump requirements in vogue at the time (16 to 18 HCP or 3½ to 4 Honor Tricks), every North would have opened 1♣. Most Easts would have passed; some would have bid 1◇, and the few who played Weak Jump Overcalls would have bid 2◇. Where East bid any number of diamonds, most North-South pairs would stop in 3♠, as North would devalue the ◇K, but where East kept silent, most Souths would reach the spade game. Against minimally adept defense, this is down one off the top after two high clubs, a club ruff and the ◇A.

Frederick, however, like most of his contemporaries, looked at his 2½ Honor Tricks and counted 15 HCP, enough for a modern 15 to 17 1NT.

East was an older woman whose vacant expression suggested that if "Twilight" were ever made into a movie, she would be welcome at the casting call. She overcalled Frederick's 1NT with 3◇. Glancing at her convention card, I saw that she and Dan were playing the Woolsey Notrump Defense, in which the only way to intervene with a long minor is to jump to the three-level. Here it proved quite effective, as it left me with a suite of unhappy alternatives including pass, double (penalty), 3♠ (game-forcing) and 4◇ (choice of majors). Ultimately I chose 3♠.

That would have propelled us to a precarious 4♠ had Fancy Dan not entered the fray with 4♣. Actually, it propelled us there nonetheless, for my illustrious partner, spurning the opportunity to pass that Dan had given him and failing to devalue his minor-suit royals, bid 4♠ anyway.

Dan led the ♣A and I glanced at his convention card to peruse the opponents' leads and carding. They were using "ace from ace-king", "third from even, low from odd" and upside-down signals. East followed with the ♣2 and I dropped the ♣J. Dan frowned at my card for a few seconds, then shifted to the ◇6. East won and tried to cash a second diamond trick, but I ruffed, drew trumps, conceded a club trick and took the rest.

Then the fun began as Dan launched into the lesson:

"As a passed hand, I couldn't have a genuine four-club bid. Four clubs had to be lead-directing with a diamond fit. Your deuce at Trick 1 showed count, not attitude, because the ♣Q was in dummy. I couldn't tell whether it was two or four, so I switched to diamonds, trusting you to return a club with a doubleton to get your ruff and beat the contract. We could have had a shared top, but instead it's another bottom," he finished in irritation.

East blinked a few times in reply, suggesting that whatever had paralyzed her cerebrum and cerebellum had not yet progressed to her medulla oblongata.

I could ignore some of Dan's errors. Never mind that he himself would be on lead against a spade contract. Never mind that his 4♣ bid took Frederick off the hook, thus undoing the good work done by East's preempt. Never mind that East's ♣2 might have been a singleton. Never mind that if East held four clubs to go along with six or seven strong diamonds, she would have bid on over four spades. And never mind that with a strong notrump behind him, reversion to standard "king from ace-king" opening leads would have made things clearer for his poor client.

However, I could not ignore the fact that Dan's 4♣ bid had thoroughly confused the distribution for East.

So, politely by human standards and subserviently by my own, I remarked, "If I were 6-4-2-1, as I might have been on the auction and early play, cashing a second diamond would be the only way to hold me to ten tricks. Otherwise I could discard dummy's losing diamond on my fourth heart."

Nonetheless, my innocuous bit of analysis enraged Dan, who immediately summoned the director.

"That infernal robot!" he complained when Deirdre arrived at the table. "Criticizing me in front of a client! How would he like it if I contradicted him in front of one of *his* clients? I demand a Zero Tolerance penalty."